PassPorter's

Treasure Hunts

at Walt Disney World
and Disney Cruise Line

Editors

Jennifer Marx

Kimberly Larner

Contributing Authors

Jennifer and Jeff Carter

PassPorter Travel Press
An imprint of MediaMarx, Inc.
P.O. Box 3880, Ann Arbor, MI 48106
http://www.passporter.com

PassPorter's® Treasure Hunts at Walt Disney World®

by Jennifer Marx, Kimberly Larner, Jennifer Carter, and Jeff Carter

© 2006 by PassPorter Travel Press, an imprint of MediaMarx, Inc.

P.O. Box 3880, Ann Arbor, Michigan 48106
877-929-3273 (order or business-related calls only, please)
Visit us on the World Wide Web at http://www.passporter.com

Special Sales: PassPorter Travel Press publications are available at special discounts for bulk purchases for sales premiums or promotions. Special editions, including personalized covers and excerpts of existing guides, can be created in large quantities. For information, write to Special Sales, P.O. Box 3880, Ann Arbor, Michigan, 48106.

Distributed by Publishers Group West.

ISBN-13: 978-1-58771-026-1
ISBN-10: 1-58771-026-9

10 9 8 7 6 5 4 3 2 1

Printed and bound in the U.S.A.

Table of Contents

3

The Treasure Team

Jennifer Marx is the editor and instigator of this little book, as well as the author of the popular PassPorter guidebooks to Walt Disney World, Disneyland, and the Disney Cruise Line. She and her husband Dave are fascinated by every aspect of the Disney theme park experience and, over the years, have created "treasure" hunts
in the parks for family and friends, and as private challenges to each other. Jennifer lives in Ann Arbor, Michigan, with Dave and their son Alexander.

Kimberly Larner, assistant editor, has a magical way with words, creating clear and concise clues for our treasure hunts. She is Jennifer's sister and one of the "pixies" at PassPorter Travel Press, sharing her sister's love of Walt Disney World. If you meet her, ask about her spur-of-the-moment Disney honeymoon (and whether her leg cast got
in the way). She lives in Charlotte, Michigan, with her husband Chad and her two charming daughters, Megan and Natalie.

Jennifer and Jeff Carter are the contributing authors of this book, as well as passionate fans of Walt Disney World who moved to Florida several years ago. Over the years, they've developed a reputation among Disney World fans for creating
fiendishly difficult, all-day, all-parks, all-resorts scavenger hunts around Walt Disney World for gatherings of Internet-based theme park fans. If there's a stone to be turned at Walt Disney World, they've found it and figured out a way to write it into a clue. When not enjoying Walt Disney World as a "civilian," Jeff works at a major Central Florida theme park. Jen and Jeff live at Walt Disney World and reside near Tampa, Florida.

Special thanks to...
Field Research and Support: Dave Marx
Mousy Mindbogglers: Debra Martin Koma, Deb Wills, and AllEarsNet.com
Office Managers and Research Wizards: Nicole Larner and Chad Larner
Proofreader: Sandy Zilka
Printer: Malloy Incorporated in Ann Arbor, MI
Online Promotions and Newsletter Editor: Sara Varney
Visibility Specialists: Kate and Doug Bandos, KSB Promotions

Treasure Map

drawn by Captain Jack Skatt

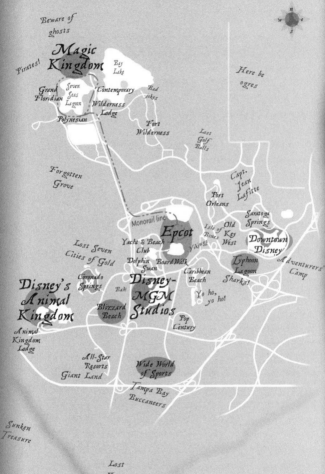

Beware of ghosts

Pirates!

Magic Kingdom

Bay Lake

Here be ogres

Grand Floridian

Seven Seas Lagoon

Contemporary

Bad jokes

Wilderness Lodge

Polynesian

Fort Wilderness

Lost Golf Balls

Forgotten Grove

Capt. Jean Lafitte

Port Orleans

Isle of Bones

Old Key West

Saratoga Springs

Monorail line

Epcot

Downtown Disney

Lost Seven Cities of Gold

Yacht & Beach Club

Vikings

Typhoon Lagoon

Dolphin Swan

BoardWalk

Adventurers' Camp

Coronado Springs

Disney-MGM Studios

Caribbean Beach

Sharky!

Disney's Animal Kingdom

Rafi

Blizzard Beach

Yo ho, yo ho!

Animal Kingdom Lodge

Pop Century

All-Star Resorts

Giant Land

Wide World of Sports

Tampa Bay Buccaneers

Sunken Treasure

Lost Keys

Disney Wonder

Disney Magic

Castaway Cay

Here be dragons

Caribbean Sea

Snorkel for Sunken Treasure

A Secret Treasure

Dear fellow hunters:

Congratulations! You've discovered my secret, hidden letter on the back of your treasure map. The paper upon which this letter is printed has a special coating that reveals itself only to true treasure hunters. Everyone else sees a dedication to my husband, Dave Marx, for his love, support, and yummy Chicken Scarpariello (thanks, honey!).

I have a secret to share with you. There's something extraordinary hidden in plain view at Walt Disney World. It's a legacy from Walt Disney, a gift from the Imagineers. It's sometimes known as THEME or STORY, and it's everywhere you look at Disney. Details big and small are just waiting to be discovered. Most people never notice them, dashing from ride to ride, trying to pack in as much as they can. But you are different, aren't you? You found this book and read my letter. You can see beyond the E-Ticket attractions. You will discover that Seumm Yett is a missing person from the Jungle Cruise, that Mickey Mouse has left behind his shorts at the Muppet hotel, and that the stained glass in Belle's hidden library tells her story.

I must confess that I love finding these hidden details even more than going on the latest and greatest rides. There's something magical about discovering a chapter in a story, a piece of the puzzle, or a totally silly bit of trivia. From my very first trip as a child, I was enchanted by the magical details—it's not Dumbo I remember, but the lights in Cinderella's windows and the smoking volcano in Mexico. Even now, after countless trips, I still discover new treasure during my visits, and I'm astounded that so much has been "hidden" for me to find.

I know your hunts will be as fruitful, your treasure as wonderful. The World is yours. Go out and discover it!

Happy hunting!

Jennifer Marx
Editor and Instigator

Calling All Treasure Hunters

You peer into the quiet interior of the old alleyway, your heart pounding in your chest. It's here somewhere, you just know it! You catch a glimpse of other treasure hunters in the distance—you must find the treasure before they do. You scan the crevices and nooks of the alleyway, checking carefully for your hidden treasure. Consulting the dog-eared journal clutched in your sweaty hand, you read that you must discover the year that the Elias Disney contracting company was established. Suddenly, you notice an unusual window that could hold the answer to your mystery. Ah, you're so close to the answer now, you can almost taste it. As a train whistles in the distance, you step closer and stare intently at the window. The lettering on the glass reveals that the contracting company was established in ... AHA! You've found your treasure—the answer to the first question on your treasure hunt. And along the way, you discovered a lovingly created yet nearly forgotten detail in the vastness that is Walt Disney World. Welcome to a new and exciting way to explore and enjoy the most magical places on earth—treasure hunting at Walt Disney World and aboard the Disney Cruise Line.

What Is Treasure Hunting?

Perhaps you remember the adventure in the blockbuster movie, "National Treasure," during which Nicolas Cage and his friends hunt for lost treasure with clues found on the back of the Declaration of Independence and the U.S. dollar bill. Or you may recall a scavenger hunt played in school or as a team-building activity at work. Disney itself has gotten into the act with hunts for its annual passholders and, most recently, to promote its Virtual Magic Kingdom game. Whether it's called a "challenge," a "scavenger hunt," or a "treasure hunt," it's all much the same idea—use your wits to find items of interest. You can hunt alone for the thrill of chasing down trivia or compete with family, friends, or even total strangers for the joy of winning. People of all ages and walks of life can get into the act and have a great time!

Where's Disney's Treasure?

Thanks to Disney's famous attention to detail, Disney offers some of the best treasure hunting grounds in the world. Delightful details are everywhere you turn in their theme parks and aboard their cruise ships, and most people completely overlook them in their dash from place to place. Even better is the fact that this treasure stays put for visitors to discover over and over, taking home only the memories and satisfaction of a good hunt!

Our treasure hunt experts—Jennifer and Jeff Carter—have scoured Walt Disney World and the Disney Cruise Line for some of the most interesting, unusual, and odd details you'll find anywhere. Your challenge is to find these details using the information in this book. Editors Jennifer Marx and Kimberly Larner organized this "treasure" into more than 100 distinct hunts that can be combined to form more elaborate challenges. Just for fun, we've thrown in fun Mousy Mindbogglers by Debra Martin Koma at AllEarsNet.com and clever clues and tall tales from Captain Skatt, our resident treasure hunter. All questions, clues, riddles, and photos lead to treasure somewhere at Walt Disney World or on the Disney Cruise Line.

Using Our Treasure Hunts

We organized this book with the treasure hunter in mind. Here are the step-by-step directions to happy hunting:

1. Choose a place. Use the table of contents on page 3 to zoom in on the location in which you want to hunt. Each park, land, resort hotel, and cruise ship is represented in these pages.

2. Choose your skill level. Use this key to difficulty level:

✠ = Easy; appropriate for new or young hunters (ages 6 & up); all answers are found without riding attractions (we also tried to put the questions in the order you would encounter them).

✠✠ = Mixed; appropriate for average adult, teen, or bright child; answers are found both on and off attractions (we identify the attraction-based questions by highlighting their numbers like this: MS-24.) In this book, we define an attraction by whether it has a queue and/or turnstile to pass through.

✠✠✠ = Expert; appropriate for veteran visitors who are very observant; answers are found both on and off attractions (but we do not always identify attraction-based questions for added difficulty).

Using Our Treasure Hunts (continued)

3. Choose a hunting method:

Play-as-You-Go Hunt: Casual hunting to enhance your overall Disney experience. Read the questions before you set out and watch for the answers as you go about your day. This is good for those who prefer not to compete, but you can still compete if you wish—just compare answers at the end of the day or the end of the trip.

Show-Your-Stuff Hunt: Compete against family or friends in an all-out hunt. Choose your competition (i.e., individuals or teams) and the scope of your hunt (i.e., just the Easy questions in Adventureland or all questions in DinoLand, U.S.A.), and set a time limit and reliable meeting place (you'll want to allow about one hour per page) and a prize (such as a souvenir or meal). Also decide how to score answers—we suggest you award one point for Easy questions, two points for Mixed, and three points for Expert. Consider a tie-breaker, such as speed or a particularly difficult question.

Free-as-a-Bird Hunt: Hunt by yourself and on your own terms. For added fun, we recommend you set a goal and a reward if you make it, such as "I will treat myself to a Dole Whip if I get ten answers correct."

4. On your mark, get set, hunt! As you go, keep your eyes peeled for answers. When you find an answer, immediately write it on the dotted line beneath the question. Be as detailed as you can. We also suggest you also note the answer's location in case there is any doubt or confusion later.

5. When finished hunting, you'll find the answers in the "locked" treasure chests in the back of this book. Carefully slit the chest open at the perforation to view the answers—match the question's letter-number code to its answer. The answers are set in a small type size to inhibit peeking or accidental reading.

Hunt Tips and Tricks

Wear comfortable shoes and sunblock. Blisters and burns are party poopers.

Use a pencil so you can make corrections. We suggest a retractable, mechanical pencil for safety and convenience.

Before you begin a hunt, read all questions carefully—twice! If you're working on Mixed and/or Expert questions, make some educated guesses as to where the answers may lie and then map out an efficient route. If you're competing with others, decide together when it is okay to read the questions (i.e, before you leave home or immediately after the hunt begins).

Keep in mind that some questions are on attractions with height restrictions. If this is a concern, avoid attraction-based questions or, if you're tall enough, use the "chicken exit" so you can enter the queue but exit before boarding.

Hunt Etiquette

The difference between a good hunter and a great hunter isn't speed or accuracy—it's simple manners! A great hunter is considerate of those around him/her. Here is the Treasure Hunter Code of Ethics:

1. Be mindful of other guests and show common courtesy. Do not run, cut in line, block walkways, enter non-guest areas, or violate posted safety warnings and notices. Show common courtesy to fellow guests. Do not hinder others' enjoyment.

2. Find all answers on your own. Do not ask a cast member or exiting guest for the answer to an attraction-based question. You may, however, ask a cast member general navigation questions, such as "Which way is the Mombasa Marketplace?" Be considerate to cast members—they've earned our respect.

3. If you meet another PassPorter treasure hunter out "in the field," you are free to greet them and volunteer one of your answers. Please do not ask another hunter for answers, however—answers can only be volunteered, not requested. If you volunteer an answer, you may accept an answer in return without violating our code of ethics.

4. Please understand that the PassPorter team cannot provide hints for questions via e-mail or the phone. If you cannot find an answer and believe there is an error, you may report it to us at http://www.passporter.com/hunts/correct.htm.

5. Take nothing, leave nothing.

6. No cheating. It's dishonorable. Enough said.

Captain's Corner

Speaking of etiquette, allow us to introduce Captain Jack Skatt, a fellow treasure hunter and Disney aficianado. The Captain is famous for his big find in 1971—the Lost Isle of Auriculus. After his archrival Professor Knott beat him to some treasure through trickery, he retired to spend more time with his family. During a trip to Walt Disney World with his nieces and nephews, he marveled at the delightful details hidden in plain sight throughout the resort ... and best of all, this treasure could not be stolen away! While examining one particularly interesting wall decoration, he stumbled across a cleverly hidden clue that he believes will lead him to the greatest find of his life. He now lives at Walt Disney World and spends his days hunting his treasure. His journal notes appear throughout this book, offering clues, tips, and a spot o' fun. He's even squirreled away a treasure hunt somewhere in this book. You can address him at captain@passporter.com.

Challenge Me!

Need more challenge? Here are ways you can use this book or other resources for more Disney fun!

✘ Mix it up! Copy the questions from every land in a single park, cut out each question so it is on its own piece of paper, put the questions in a hat, and draw! Now you don't always know in what land you'll find the answers to a question.

✘ Make it a digital photo hunt! Take photos of your answers as you go—it increases difficulty and the time required.

✘ Collect stuff! Throw in a few extra challenges, such as collecting autographs from certain characters, guide maps, or whatever interests you.

✘ Challenge your friends or family to a day of treasure hunting against one another. The losers treat the winner to dinner!

✘ Amuse yourself before or after a trip by trying to answer the questions at home. Tip: Many of the Easy questions can be answered using articles, photos, and trip reports available on the Internet! Google will be your best friend.

✘ Play Captain Skatt's hidden treasure hunt. (Captain Skatt is introduced on the previous page.)

✘ Enter the PassPorter Earn-Your-Badge Treasure Hunt to earn your authentic "Treasure Hunter" pin.

✘ Join us at our annual MouseFest event for PassPorter treasure hunts, as well as scavenger hunts, trivia hunts, mini MouseAdventures, and "Great Races" by fellow Disney fans. Visit http://www.mousefest.org for more information.

✘ Check to see if Disney has any of its own treasure hunts going on—just ask fellow fans on the PassPorter message board. Visit http://www.passporterboards.com.

✘ Go geocaching at Disney! Geocaching is treasure hunting with GPS (Global Positioning Systems) units. For more information, visit http://www.geocaching.com and read our informative article on Disney geocaching at http://www.passporter.com/news/news050205.htm.

✘ Make your own treasure hunts for your personal use or to share with others! See our tips on page 148.

✘ Hunt for corrections to the treasure hunts in this book! Disney is constantly changing, which means answers will go missing or be changed. If you find a correction, send us a clear explanation, along with the suggested change (and a digital photo, if possible). If you are the first to correct a question and we can verify your corrections, you will receive a free copy of the next edition! (Limit one book per person.) Visit http://www.passporter.com/hunts/correct.htm.

A Disney Surprise!
Home Sweet Home

✠

Enjoy this little treasure hunt in your own home to get excited for your upcoming Disney trip! Or use it to surprise someone you love with the news of a trip or a copy of this book. Just write each clue on a piece of paper and hide it in the location indicated in parentheses after the clue. Present the first clue to the hunter(s) to start the hunt! Have fun!

1. You're going to need comfortable shoes to get where we're going. Find your favorite pair of shoes.

2. A good hat is like a good friend—they've always got you covered. Find the place we keep our hats.
(Hide this clue with shoes.)

3. You'll want a solid meal before our adventure. Find the place we keep our food fresh.
(Hide this clue in your coat closet or with hats.)

4. Money, money, who's got the money? We need money! Find the place we keep our money.
(Hide this clue in your refrigerator.)

5. A box won't do—we need a suitcase, too! Find our biggest suitcase.
(Hide this clue with a wallet, purse, or piggy bank.)

6. A little pixie says we need some dust. Find the dustiest place in the house!
(Hide this clue in your biggest suitcase.)

7. The Big Cheese gets a lot of fan mail. Do you have any mail? Find the place we get our mail.
(Hide this clue under a bed or some other dusty spot.)

(Write this on a postcard, complete it with your personal message, and put it in your mailbox.)
"Oh boy! You've found the treasure! Way to go!"
(Your personal message here.)

Magic Kingdom's
Main Street, U.S.A.

"Explore a town square and train station—you'll need your wits and imagination!"—Captain Skatt's journal, volume 1

MS-1. How much is a game of football at the train station?

....

MS-2. How many trains appear in the mural "Spanning the Continent" at the train station?

....

MS-3. Which two presidents have portraits in City Hall?

....

MS-4. What number is City Hall on the braille map?

....

MS-5. What initials are on the feed buckets in the Firehouse?

....

MS-6. Where can you get your hair cut?

....

MS-7. How much does the heaviest barbell weigh on the rack in the Main Street Athletic Club?

....

MS-8. In what year was Casey's Corner established?

....

MS-9. How many runs did Mudville score in the third inning?

....

MS-10. Who hosts the Baby Care Center?

....

MS-11. Which buffet has character?

....

MS-12. What is in the heart on the sidewalk outside of Tony's Town Square Restaurant?

....

MS-13. Does Goofy have a flower on his coat outside of Exposition Hall?

....

Magic Kingdom's
Main Street, U.S.A.

✠ ✠

MS-14. Where is the Art Festival?

MS-15. Who was the voice of Baloo in the original Jungle Book?

MS-16. Who's the headmaster of the Fire Academy?

MS-17. On what field does Mudville play?

MS-18. For what did Walt receive an Honorable Mention from the Academy of Motion Picture Arts and Sciences?

MS-19. The Main Street Athletic Club is home to which team?

MS-20. What's the motto of the Dreamers and Doers Development Company?

MS-21. What type of engine is the Lilly Belle?

MS-22. What baking powder is advertised in the Marketplace?

MS-23. In what year did the Main Street Athletic Club win the Rowing Championship?

MS-24. How many bells are on the wall next to the fireman's pole in the Firehouse?

MS-25. "Big Six" Matthewson drinks what?

MS-26. What three services are only available to members at the AAA Service Provider Kiosk?

Magic Kingdom's
Main Street, U.S.A.
✠ ✠ ✠

MS-27. How many miles east of Sacramento City is Promontory Point?

....

MS-28. Who makes the Jack Rose toilet water?

....

MS-29. You should you treat your friends to what company's special tricks?

....

MS-30. Who is the supervisor of the Turkish baths?

....

MS-31. Who made the photo stamp in the upstairs train station ticket booth?

....

MS-32. In what year was Elias Disney's Contracting Company established?

....

MS-33. What are the only type of rolls you can use in the player piano/music box upstairs in the Main Street Train Station?

....

MS-34. What magic item does Lucky Tiger make?

....

MS-35. Who makes the baseballs in the basket on top of the Coca-Cola boxes in Casey's Corner?

....

MS-36. Whose carriage company is located at 57 Church Street?

....

Captain's Corner

In dire need of a thorough cleansing after a long day of treasure hunting, I searched high and low for the entrance to the famed Turkish baths. I eventually settled for a double chocolate chip muffin. I reckon I could have just climbed through the window.

Magic Kingdom's
Adventureland

"Wonders and treasure await you here, see pirates of old and the birds of fame; explore the jungle river and fly in carpets—adventure is calling your name!"—Captain Jack Skatt's journal

AL-1. What musical instrument do you see and hear as you cross the bridge to Adventureland from the hub?

AL-2. What family lives in the huge tree?

AL-3. What are the camels doing to Aladdin's carpets?

AL-4. What is Zazu the hornbill holding on the main Enchanted Tiki Room sign?

AL-5. Where can you drive a miniature Bomokandi Bertha or Zambesi Zelda boat?

AL-6. How many ships sail underneath the Zanzibar Trading Company sign?

AL-7. What will you find in the Fuente de Fortuna?

AL-8. What is unusual about the Jolly Roger skull and crossbones flag flying near the entrance to the Pirates of the Caribbean?

AL-9. Who sings "Yo ho, yo ho, a parrot's life for me!"

AL-10. Who is pictured on the El Pirata Y el Perico sign?

AL-11. What do the tiki statues shown below do?

Magic Kingdom's
Adventureland

✠ ✠

AL-12. When did the Swiss Family Robinson wreck their ship?

AL-13. Why don't the Tiki birds get out much?

AL-14. According to the skeleton at the beginning of Pirates of the Caribbean, dead men tell no what?

AL-15. Who would use the restroom marked Caballeros?

AL-16. According to Zazu, who turned out the lights in the Tiki Room?

AL-17. How many guys are climbing the totem pole on the Jungle Cruise in order to escape the charging rhino?

AL-18. How many times does your boat "drop" in Pirates of the Caribbean?

AL-19. Who are you trying to wake up at the beginning of Tiki Room?

AL-20. In the right queue of Pirates of the Caribbean, examine the first cannon you reach. What shape is the stack of cannonballs?

AL-21. How many people are trying to escape the jail at the end of Pirates of the Caribbean?

AL-22. How many tigers are in the temple when your Jungle Cruise enters the Mekong river?

AL-23. What are the names of the four main birds in the Tiki Room (not Iago or Zazu)?

Magic Kingdom's
Adventureland

✠ ✠ ✠

AL-24. What time is high tide according to the sign outside Island Supply?

AL-25. Carlos is told to not be what animal?

AL-26. On the Jungle Cruise, you see an explorer getting a rhino horn in his nether regions. What is in the red can on his pack?

AL-27. In the Jungle Cruise queue, there are 72 units of what above the 12 cases of arachnid sedative?

AL-28. How many cannons on the pirate ship are attacking the fort in Pirates of the Caribbean?

AL-29. According to their menu, what is being served to the Jungle Cruise staff on Friday?

AL-30. Who is the Jungle Cruise employee of the month?

AL-31. Where is the Elephant Safari Company from?

AL-32. What is the maximum seating at El Pirata y el Perico?

AL-33. In what city is Eva's Exotic Plant Emporium?

AL-34. Who intends to go to the Hall of Presidents for a nap?

AL-35. Where is the birdhouse pictured to the right?

Magic Kingdom's
Frontierland

✠

"A pioneering spirit puts you in good stead to explore the mines, mountains, and bears; but watch out for old Texas John as he is quite a scare."—From Captain Skatt's letter to Pecos Bill

FR-1. How many rifles are in the Frontierland Shootin' Arcade sign?

....

FR-2. What color is the canteen on top of the Frontierland Shootin' Arcade?

....

FR-3. What is roosting in the big tree inside Frontierland Shootin' Arcade?

....

FR-4. What is trail boss John Slaughter's nickname?

....

FR-5. What year was Grizzly Hall (the home of the Country Bear Jamboree) founded?

....

FR-6. What year was the saloon established?

....

FR-7. What is the name of the river that runs through Frontierland?

....

FR-8. What mill is on Tom Sawyer Island?

....

FR-9. Near Splash Mountain are statues of Brer Bear and Brer Fox searching for Brer Rabbit. Where is Brer Rabbit hiding in this scene?

....

FR-10. What time is it according to Brer Rabbit's clock in the Briar Patch?

....

FR-11. What is the name of the children's playground near the exit of Splash Mountain?

....

FR-12. Where is Cactus Canyon?

....

Magic Kingdom's
Frontierland

✠ ✠

FR-13. According to his tombstone, what did Ol' Tom Hubbard die from?

FR-14. The heads of how many animals are mounted on the wall of the Country Bear Jamboree theater?

FR-15. What's Brer Goose's fishing line in his portrait?

FR-16. What color of long johns is the man wearing in the bathtub on Big Thunder Mountain Railroad?

FR-17. What color star is on the signed boots from Buffalo Bill in Pecos Bills?

FR-18. What is the note of the Jug that Ted is playing in the Country Bear Jamboree?

FR-19. What color of feather boa is Teddy wearing?

FR-20. There's a bag of flour and what else on the left side of the first hill on Splash Mountain?

FR-21. What color is Brer Rabbit's shirt?

FR-22. What color tutu is the bear in the Country Bear Jamboree lobby wearing?

FR-23. What instrument does Henry the bear play?

FR-24. Who's whistling at the end of Splash Mountain with Brer Rabbit?

FR-25. What is S.S. Bedard? (Hint: See MS-36.)

FR-26. If you hit a bull's-eye in the Boothill sign, what happens?

Magic Kingdom's
Frontierland

✠ ✠ ✠

FR-27. How many heads of choice stock are on auction at the Kane Auction Yard on Saturday?

FR-28. What does Beehive Realtors have for rent?

FR-29. What is the last name of the Country Bear known as Liverlips?

FR-30. Who autographed a pair of white gloves for Billy?

FR-31. Lucky #13 is the name of what in the Frontierland Shootin' Arcade?

FR-32. What kind of moonshine is on Splash Mountain?

FR-33. When did Ruthless Billy Jack meet his maker?

FR-34. What does Brer Rabbit say Brer Bear is going to get from the Laughing Place?

FR-35. What is the Code of the West?

FR-36. Why can't you run away from trouble?

FR-37. According to Brer Fox, Brer Rabbit isn't going to do much what at his Laughing Place?

FR-38. What's the name of Davy Crockett's first rifle?

Captain's Corner

Old Pecos Bill and I love to swap tales. I recently told him the story of how little Slue Foot Susie signed her black boots for me.

Magic Kingdom's
Liberty Square

✠

"The pursuit of liberty leads to a grand old tree; then on to presidents, riverboats, and mansions—oh what harmony!"—From Captain Skatt's love poem to Madame Leota

LS-1. What number house/door is between Sleepy Hollow and the Heritage House?

LS-2. How many flag poles surround the Liberty Bell replica?

LS-3. Does the replica of the Liberty Bell have a crack in it?

LS-4. Who sponsors Yankee Traders?

LS-5. What year appears on the Trail Creek Traders shop?

LS-6. Counting both sides, how many lanterns are on the Liberty Tree Tavern sign?

LS-7. How many men are in the boat on the Columbia Harbour House sign?

LS-8. What shape is the lock on the well outside Haunted Mansion?

LS-9. What is the name of the riverboat?

LS-10. Where is the rocking horse pictured below?

Magic Kingdom's
Liberty Square
✠ ✠

LS-11. How many candles are on the moving coffin?

LS-12. How many globes are on stage with the presidents?

LS-13. How many hitchhiking ghosts are there?

LS-14. Ichabod Crane does what kind of lessons by appointment?

LS-15. "No mourning please" is the request of whom?

LS-16. On July 8, 1835, for whom did the Liberty Bell ring?

LS-17. What color flowers is the bride holding in the attic?

LS-18. What fell on Fred's head?

LS-19. What kind of animal is spinning a web on the staircase going up in the Haunted Mansion?

LS-20. What state ratified the Constitution on January 2, 1788?

LS-21. What year appears on Colonial Hall?

LS-22. What year did Rover die?

LS-23. Complete this sentence: "Past this gateway stirs
_ __ _____ _____ __ __ _____."

LS-24. What lovely lady offers seances, potions, and crystal gazing?

Magic Kingdom's
Liberty Square
✠ ✠ ✠

LS-25. What sheet music is above the sheet music for The Holly and the Ivy?

LS-26. How many Grim Grinning Ghosts are there?

LS-27. Dear Beloved George has what through his head?

LS-28. What color are the cat's eyes in the opening hall portraits on Haunted Mansion?

LS-29. What is seen burning while riding the riverboat?

LS-30. Who did in Bluebeard?

LS-31. What kind of tree is the Liberty Tree?

LS-32. Complete this sequence: pear, _____, grape, pear

LS-33. What color undershirt does the knight in the endless hallway wear on Haunted Mansion?

LS-34. Which founding father, not a president, is seen in a portrait as you exit the Hall of Presidents?

LS-35. What TV station is present in the Hall of Presidents?

Captain's Corner

Lady Leota has stolen my heart! Not only do I hear music when she speaks, but I see her face illuminated with the fruits of my love. She is particularly fetching in cherry. I just know that if we could be together forever we'd have a ball!

Magic Kingdom's
Fantasyland
✠

"Teacups spin and elephants twirl—have you ever seen such a fantastic world? Look about for treasure galore, for it's a small world no more!"—Captain Skatt's journal entry for Feb. 29

FL-1. What colors are the wicked stepsisters' faces when Cinderella is trying on the slipper in the castle's mural?

....

FL-2. What is painted in gold on Cinderella's fountain?

....

FL-3. What store has a beanstalk growing out of it?

....

FL-4. What shape is the pavement near the Sword in the Stone?

....

FL-5. What color are the flags above Cinderella's Golden Carrousel?

....

FL-6. What creatures are cavorting atop Cinderella's Golden Carrousel sign?

....

FL-7. Cinderella's favorite horse on the Carrousel has a gold ribbon in its tail—what color is this horse's bridle?

....

FL-8. According to the sign, how many dwarfs are there?

....

FL-9. What color is Pooh's shirt?

....

FL-10. What character is upside down in the Many Adventures of Winnie the Pooh sign?

....

FL-11. Where is Piglet in Pooh's Playful Spot?

....

FL-12. What is Dormouse popping out of at the Mad Tea Party?

....

FL-13. What Disney princess visits the Fairytale Garden regularly?

....

Magic Kingdom's
Fantasyland
✠ ✠

FL-14. On the Wishing Well, what does the plaque at the base read?

FL-15. What is on the head of the heffalump that blows smoke rings?

FL-16. What animal is on the stairs of the dwarfs' house?

FL-17. Who hands Donald the sorceror's hat in Mickey's PhilharMagic?

FL-18. What are the names of the seven rooms in the Pinocchio Village Haus?

FL-19. In what chapter do you join Pooh and his friends on a very blustery day?

FL-20. Who's Goofy looking for at the beginning of Mickey's PhilharMagic?

FL-21. What colors are painted on the hot air balloon on Dumbo?

FL-22. Who almost bounces right out of the ride at the Many Adventures of Winnie the Pooh?

FL-23. How many buzzards are in the branch as you enter the outdoor scene with the queen/witch?

FL-24. How many mermaids are in the lagoon on Peter Pan's Flight?

FL-25. What color napkin is tied around Donald's neck during Be Our Guest?

FL-26. What color is Wendy's nightgown?

Magic Kingdom's
Fantasyland
✠ ✠ ✠

FL-27. What time is it on Big Ben on Peter Pan's Flight?

....

FL-28. What two figures represent the United States in "it's a small world"?

....

FL-29. What kind of animal is Nana?

....

FL-30. Where is the Floody Place?

....

FL-31. Who is in the top left keyhole of the dresser in Tinker Bell's Treasure?

....

FL-32. What animal can be found on the pink and white teepee on the load area of Peter Pan's Flight?

....

FL-33. What's the last instrument Donald takes out?

....

FL-34. Translate this: La Fontaine de Cendrillon

....

FL-35. Where can the words, "Caution! Doors Open Magically Toward You" be found?

....

FL-36. Huffalumps and woozles steal what?

....

FL-37. What song is the orchestra playing that irritates Donald so much?

....

FL-38. Besides the Poison Apple spell, what other spell is visible in the Queen's spell book?

....

FL-39. The Nites Inn requests what?

....

FL-40. What two dolls are having tea at the beginning of Peter Pan's Flight?

....

Magic Kingdom's
Mickey's Toontown Fair

✠

"What do two mouse houses, a duck dinghy, and a pup plane make? An amazing cartoon world, for Pete's sake!"—From Captain Skatt's holiday card, 2004

TT-1. Who's the judge on the Toontown Fair sign?

....

TT-2. What is Pete holding above his garage?

....

TT-3. What is floating in the Gas Gulp Pump at Pete's Garage?

....

TT-4. What is the license plate on the blue car in front of Pete's Garage?

....

TT-5. What color bumpers are in Pete's bumper crop?

....

TT-6. What props up Goofy's mailbox?

....

TT-7. What color is the roof at Mickey's Country House?

....

TT-8. Who is the founder of Mickey's Toontown Fair?

....

TT-9. Who's the Captain of the Miss Daisy?

....

TT-10. What shape is in the center of each blue ribbon on the Toontown Train Station?

....

TT-11. Where will you find these ducks?

....

....

Magic Kingdom's
Mickey's Toontown Fair

✠ ✠

TT-12. Who wants you to trust him with your car?

TT-13. Maxwell Mouse Coffee is what?

TT-14. What two schools have flags on Mickey's couch?

TT-15. What sea is on the map in Donald's boat?

TT-16. What are the settings on the stove in the remodeling kitchen contest?

TT-17. What is the name of Donald's boat?

TT-18. What kind of pencil is on Minnie's desk?

TT-19. What's the slogan of Pete's Paint Shop and Body?

TT-20. How many keys are on Mickey's keychain in his foyer?

TT-21. What Florida license plate is in Mickey's shed?

TT-22. Who is winning the Ping Pong tournament at Mickey's?

TT-23. What color is Minnie's sewing machine?

Captain's Corner

I visited my pal Mick at his country estate today. After regaling him with my adventure on Mt. Mayday, he told me about his glory days in school. It seems he was quite the crack-up at Duckberg U, where he loved to pull pranks on his rivals at Goofey Tech.

Magic Kingdom's
Mickey's Toontown Fair

✠ ✠ ✠

TT-24. Who's the Rowdiest Rooster on Radio?

TT-25. Who invented Mirthaid?

TT-26. What kind of honor is citizenship in Toontown?

TT-27. What are the 8:00 am classes offered at the Barnstormer?

TT-28. What brand of overalls does Mickey wear?

TT-29. What are three of Goofy's cash crops?

TT-30. Who is reading Wuthering Mice?

TT-31. What did Prof. Ludwig Von Drake do on the S.S. Daisy?

TT-32. Where will you find that "1 smidgen = 4 oodges"?

TT-33. Who are Minnie's great-grandparents?

TT-34. Who are Mickey's pen pals?

TT-35. Who joined Troop 71?

TT-36. Where is the "Palm Tree"?

TT-37. For what did Minnie win a Baking Award?

TT-38. Where is the sign pictured below?

Magic Kingdom's
Tomorrowland

✠

"Yesterday's fantasy is today's Progress; this is not really Tomorrow, I must confess."—Excerpt from Captain Skatt's speech at the grand opening of the Blue Line Station at Perfect Park Acres

TO-1. What is the slogan of the Tomorrowland Power and Light Company?

TO-2. What's the name of the avenue between the end of Main Street, U.S.A. and Rockettower Plaza?

TO-3. Where is the Prisoner Transport Center?

TO-4. What color is the nose cone on an Astro Orbiter rocket ship?

TO-5. What two characters appear on the sign over the door for Buzz Lightyear's Space Ranger Spin?

TO-6. What color hat is the Robo News Robot wearing?

TO-7. How many gears make up the Carousel of Progress sign?

TO-8. In what mode is the Cool Ship?

TO-9. How many lanes wide is the Tomorrowland Indy Speedway?

TO-10. What number is on the racing car in front of the Tomorrowland Indy Speedway?

TO-11. The positions of how many cars can be displayed on the scoring tower at the speedway?

TO-12. Where is the Metropolis Science Centre?

Magic Kingdom's
Tomorrowland

✠ ✠

TO-13. As she's preparing for her halloween date in the Carousel of Progress, Patty is using an exercise machine that was originally from what decade?

TO-14. What is the age recommendation for Play Clay?

TO-15. What experiment number is Stitch?

TO-16. What is sleeping on the presents at Grandma's feet in the Christmas scene of Carousel of Progress?

TO-17 Complete this sentence spoken by the narrarator on the Tomorrowland Transit Authority: "Space Mountain makes ordinary space travel ____ ____."

TO-18. What kind of accelerator does your XP-37 Space Cruiser enter at the beginning of Buzz Lightyear's Space Ranger Spin?

TO-19. Which Tomorrowland Transit Authority Line crosses above the walkway at the entrance to Space Mountain?

TO-20. What does the Magic 8-Ball predict in the Buzz Lightyear queue?

TO-21. To what U.S. state does Stitch make his Great Escape?

TO-22. In Buzz Lightyear's Space Ranger Spin, on what channel is the giant baby monitor?

TO-23. What are turkey legs called at the Lunching Pad?

Magic Kingdom's
Tomorrowland

✠ ✠

TO-24. According to the map in the Buzz Lightyear queue, what planet is in Sector 6?

TO-25. What does Tom Morrow need to do for his party from Saturn?

TO-26. How many three-eyed aliens are atop the small gift shop at the exit of Buzz Lightyear?

TO-27. In the 1920s scene of Carousel of Progress, what Chinese restaurant can be seen out the window?

TO-28. How many batteries are in the Star Command Power Center?

TO-29. The junior cadet training cruise is what type of Space Cruiser?

TO-30. How many "palm trees" are at the entrance to Space Mountain?

TO-31. According to the lead character in Carousel of Progress, what is the new name for Sasparilla?

TO-32. What attraction is "Tomorrowland's gateway to the galaxy"?

TO-33. Who keeps the water in the drip pan from overflowing on Carousel of Progress?

TO-34. What prisoner classification level is Stitch?

TO-35. Who keeps interrupting when Sara is interrupting in the Carousel of Progress?

TO-36. How many launch controllers are in Space Mountain's Alpha Launch Control?

Tomorrowland

✠ ✠ ✠

TO-37. 40 MV of power equates to what color?

TO-38. According to a note found in the Carousel of Progress, who called wanting changes?

TO-39. Blue is what type of power level on Zurg's secret weapon?

TO-40. Coca-Cola's Standard Transgalactic Delivery can only be opened in what kind of atmosphere?

TO-41. Pleakley has a sticker from what resort on the back of his suitcase?

TO-42. What brand of stove is in the beginning-of-the-century scene on Carousel of Progress?

TO-43. What can you have done in five minutes while waiting for a train?

TO-44. What is the greatest invention of all time?

TO-45. What transit line services Perfect Park Acres?

TO-46. What types of suites are at the Hover Hotel?

TO-47.

AllEars® Mousy Mindboggler

Each day people pass me by as though I wasn't there
Until they hear me talk and then they stop and stare!
I'm short and nondescript, but that doesn't get me down
You can meet me in this land, just don't push me around!

Who am I?

Epcot's
Future World East

✠

"This world of the future is inspiring—its exhibits and pavilions finds minds inquiring. From the history of communication to rockets firing, a visit to Future World leaves one perspiring."
—Scrawled in the margin of one of Captain Skatt's maps

FE-1. How do you "leave a legacy" at Epcot?

....

FE-2. What organization is the recipient of contributions made at the entrance plaza's fountain in front of Spaceship Earth?

....

FE-3. What is the name of the giant geosphere?

....

FE-4. What does Spaceship Earth explore, according to signs near it?

....

FE-5. Complete this sentence: "Innovations: Road to _____ ."

....

FE-6. How often does the Fountain of Nations begin a new "water ballet" show during the day?

....

FE-7. Who makes the deep-cycle batteries that power the Solar Bench?

....

FE-8. What shape are the topiary bushes near Universe of Energy? (Be as specific as possible.)

....

FE-9. What color is the largest "planet" in the Mission: SPACE Planetary Plaza?

....

FE-10. What U.S. astronaut said, "Dare to dream..."?

....

FE-11. How many people appear on the "Flight Trainees Standby Entrance" sign at Mission:SPACE?

....

FE-12. What two teams take part in the Mission Space Race at the end of Mission:SPACE?

....

35

Epcot's
Future World East

✠

FE-13. From what location are the postcards sent at the end of Mission:SPACE?

FE-14. What playground allows junior astronauts to explore and crawl about?

FE-15. What is unusual about the shape of two of the electrical boxes in the Cargo Bay shop at the exit of Mission:SPACE?

FE-16. What is the test dummy doing in the car at Cool Wash?

FE-17. On a sign advertising the "Inside Track" outside Test Track, what time is the PM Shipment?

FE-18. What is printed on the pink note on the warning signs outside Test Track?

FE-19. At the GM Information Center, what car brand is on the leftmost sign?

FE-20. What's in the box in the garden near Test Track?

Captain's Corner

Upon returning from a legendary journey to the red orb, I encountered two ships in a heated race against one another. Each had a crew of nearly 28 persons. The ship in the lead was the Triton, and her crew worked feverishly to keep it on course. Lagging behind was the Orion. Her team tried valiantly to outrace the Triton team. As the ships flew toward land, team Orion surged ahead and proved victorious. Perhaps I shall join the crew for the next race.

Epcot's
Future World East

FE-21. How tall is the X-2 space shuttle?

FE-22. In what year did GM start the world's first automotive proving grounds?

FE-23. The ISTC celebrates 75 years of human spaceflight in what year?

FE-24. After the hill climb test, what percent downgrade does your vehicle travel?

FE-25. Where is the X-2's designated landing site?

FE-26. How many tons of pressure can the die press create at the exit of Test Track?

FE-27. Who made the first spacewalk?

FE-28. Where is GM's desert proving ground?

FE-29. In what year did Test Track open?

FE-30. What dalmatian went into space on the Expedition 205 mission?

FE-31. To where do you ride the time machine in Spaceship Earth?

FE-32. What radio station broadcasts in the theater after the dinosaur diorama on Universe of Energy?

FE-33. What two types of steel are tested in the corrosion test area in the Test Track queue?

FE-34. What is the rank of the Mission:SPACE flight director?

Epcot's
Future World East
✠ ✠

FE-35. What Roman item was turned against Rome and led to the Dark Ages?

....

FE-36. What is the largest non-adjustable wrench size on a tool rack by the "Cool Wash"?

....

FE-37. As you exit Test Track's building, the words "Thank You" appear in how many languages on the road signs?

....

FE-38. How many markers are on the "moon" in the Planetary Plaza?

....

FE-39. Why does Spaceship Earth stop intermittently?

....

FE-40. What type of engine does the X-2 Deep Space Shuttle have?

....

FE-41. Environmental test #7 is what type of test performed at Test Track?

....

FE-42. On Spaceship Earth there are a pair of monks. One is scribbling. What is the other doing?

....

FE-43. How many compartments are in the giant Gravity Wheel in the Mission:SPACE queue?

....

FE-44. According to the monitor at the end of the Test Track vehicle test, how many tests did you take?

....

FE-45. What merchants created the first common alphabet?

....

Epcot's
Future World East

✠ ✠ ✠

FE-46. Who is responsible for extending the wings and engaging hypersleep?

....

FE-47. What is the capacity of the floor jack at the very end of Test Track, on the right hand side of your car?

....

FE-48. How many miles of roads are there at Holden's automotive proving ground?

....

FE-49. What spring number do they suggest they try to see if vibration levels stay the same?

....

FE-50. What is the vertical clearance of the Test Track control tower?

....

FE-51. What was the top speed of the lunar rover?

....

FE-52. Who is pictured with the woman at West 6-A-3-10-8?

....

FE-53. What is the caveman holding in the mural as you enter Spaceship Earth?

....

FE-54. What is the one source of energy that will never run out?

....

FE-55. As you enter the road couse on Test Track, what does the very first mile marker say?

....

FE-56. How many fuel cells are filled during the X-2's preflight system diagnostics?

....

FE-57. When was the first X-2 Deep Space mission?

....

FE-58. At what college is "Stupid Judy" a professor of Energy?

....

Epcot's
Future World East

✠ ✠ ✠

FE-59. What astronaut team is scheduled for EVA training at 0800?

FE-60. What type of toolbox is found in the electromagnetic compatibility chamber?

FE-61. What fuel powers the X-2 Deep Space shuttle?

FE-62. What type of sleeve allows for the replacement of damaged road sign posts?

FE-63. What is the name of the boy videoconferencing with the young Japanese girl in Spaceship Earth?

FE-64. At the top of Spaceship Earth you enter a scene where you look down on Earth from space. What ocean is in the center of the picture of Earth?

FE-65. What is the greatest adventure in the history of mankind?

FE-66. What paper is the newsboy on Spaceship Earth selling?

FE-67. In the cold test chamber, there is a clock on an office wall. What does the clock face say?

FE-68. In the radio booth on Spaceship Earth, what station's call letters appear on the microphone?

FE-69. What was first seen in 1952 at Motorama?

FE.70. Where will you find the balloon pictured to the right?

Epcot's
Future World West

"Across the plaza lies more future fun, the seas are living and the land is Soarin'. Imagination is on the run, and there's a purple dragon. I think I need an Innovention because these puns are overdone."—Captain Skatt's journal entry on a bad hair day

FW-1. What company presents the Ultimate Home Theater Experience in Innoventions West?

FW-2. What brand of oversized balls is sold in the breezeway of Innoventions West?

FW-3. Where will you find a place that celebrates mankind's greatest inventions?

FW-4. What is unusual about the drinking fountain behind Innoventions West?

FW-5. Characters from what Pixar movie can be found in a display outside of The Living Seas?

FW-6. How many sea creatures are in the rocks to the left of The Living Seas?

FW-7. What is interesting about the rocks in front of The Living Seas?

FW-8. Monorail pylon 209 is located in front of what Epcot pavilion?

Captain's Corner

Today I dined at the Great Reef with fellow adventurers from Down Under. Dory actually remembered to show up, along with Marlin, his son Nemo, Tad, pink Pearl, Gil, and Bloat. They seemed a tad uneasy when the food arrived and left in haste for some appointment at The Rocks.

Epcot's
Future World West

FW-9. Who sponsors The Land pavilion?

....

FW-10. How many big balloons are suspended over the seating area of Sunshine Seasons in The Land?

....

FW-11. What is between the balloons in The Land?

....

FW-12. What kind of flower is above the Garden Grill sign in The Land?

....

FW-13. Where can a kid become a junior chef?

....

FW-14. What pavilion features a fountain that appears to flow backward?

....

FW-15. What color is the character peeking over the top of the Imagination! pavilion sign?

....

FW-16. Who sponsors the Imagination pavilion?

....

FW-17. What color is Figment's shirt?

....

FW-18. Where will you find the topiary pictured below? (For extra credit, name the character.)

....

Epcot's
Future World West

✠ ✠

FW-19. How many rows of teeth does Bruce the shark have on his lower jaw?

FW-20. According to a display sign in The Living Seas, what is the temperature of the Coral Reef?

FW-21. What number is the "Submouseable" found at the base of the stairs in The Living Seas pavilion?

FW-22. What is the name of Pumbaa's restaurant in the "Circle of Life" movie?

FW-23. In whose lagoon do the stingrays swim at The Living Seas?

FW-24. How do you control the music-playing Figment animations in ImageWorks?

FW-25. Over what state does Soarin' take you?

FW-26. According to Figment, what does Dr. Nigel Channing taste like?

FW-27. In Soarin', over what Disney park do you fly?

FW-28. Which inventor shrunk the audience?

FW-29. According to his door, found in the entrance to Journey Into Imagination with Figment, what is Nigel Channing's job title?

FW-30. What type of paint is found in the back of Figment's truck on Journey Into Imagination?

FW-31. What is the name of Nick's snake in "Honey, I Shrunk the Audience"?

Epcot's
Future World West

FW-32. Who said "The secret powers of nature are generally discovered unsolicited"?

FW-33. According to the film "Circle of Life," cars became the 19th-century solution to what pollution?

FW-34. What decidedly American pie scent can be found in the smell lab of Journey Into Imagination?

FW-35. What seems to scamper around your feet during "Honey, I Shrunk the Audience"?

FW-36. What is the name of the mouse that is replicated in "Honey, I Shrunk the Audience"?

FW-37. According to the Living With the Land attraction, what contains half of the Earth's life?

FW-38. What kind of fish is Gurgle from Finding Nemo?

FW-39. What is unusual about the balloon Figment is floating in during the last scene of Journey Into Imagination?

FW-40. When Figment tells you that "Imagination is a blast" at the end of Journey Into Imagination, how many ballerina puppets appear?

FW-41. Where (and what) is the Duty Roster at The Living Seas?

FW-42. What two characters break the dam at the end of the "Circle of Life" film?

FW-43. What color is Figment's suitcase when he is hopping on the imaginary train with you?

Epcot's
Future World West

✠ ✠ ✠

FW-44. In what year did Nicolaus Copernicus create his theory of a sun-centered solar system?

....

FW-45. The Civil Engineering Achievment of Merit award was bestowed upon The Living Seas in what year?

....

FW-46. What is the RFD (Rural Free Delivery) number for B. Jones?

....

FW-47. Where is Bruce's playground?

....

FW-48. What kind of fish is Tad?

....

FW-49. Where are cardinal fish eggs incubated?

....

FW-50. What marking is found on the golf ball that flies towards the camera on Soarin'?

....

FW-51.

AllEars® Mousy Mindboggler

When you dine here, you enjoy the view
Though it's not the outdoors you survey

At times it might seem things are watching YOU
Or you might see Mickey at play

Some food they serve here comes from quite nearby
It's delicious beyond belief

But it may not be to everyone's taste
They'll be asking you, "Where's the beef?"

Which Walt Disney World restaurant is this?

....

Epcot's
Future World West

✠ ✠ ✠

FW-52. What is not improved downwind of Pumbaa?

FW-53. What famous bridge is shown in the first scene of Soarin'?

FW-54. According to Timon in the "Circle of Life" what doesn't look so bad on Simba?

FW-55. What is a Moorish Idol?

FW-56. What kind of testing is in progress at the Imagination Institute's laugh lab?

FW-57. What does QED equal?

FW-58. What color is the "Figment Duckie" that can be found in Figment's bathtub?

FW-59. What color is the tile that prevents the two murals outside The Land from being a mirror image?

FW-60. Where is the image pictured below?

Epcot's
World Showcase East

"Journey around the countries of the world, where new cultures and languages are swirled. Flags from Mexico to Norway are unfurled, and in China, Germany, and Italy dancers are swirled."
—Captain Skatt's international treatise on treasures transworld

WE-1. What is on the large table in Casa Mexicana inside the Mexico pavilion?

WE-2. Where is the River of Time in the World Showcase?

WE-3. Where can you dine in twilight, even on a sunny day?

WE-4. How many U.S. mailboxes are between Mexico and Norway?

WE-5. How many dragons (full or partial) are on the roofs of the Stave Church?

WE-6. What is on the roof of the seating area beside Kringla Bakeri og Kafe?

WE-7. What colors are the sail on the Viking play ship?

WE-8. How many fingers and toes do trolls have?

WE-9. What's in the basket of the delivery bike at the Outpost?

WE-10. How many columns are in The Gate of the Golden Sun in front of the China pavilion?

WE-11. How many stars are in China's flag?

WE-12. What minority is solid yellow on the national minorities of the People's Republic of China map?

Epcot's
World Showcase East

✠

WE-13. What is the St. George statue battling in Germany?

WE-14. What is above the water fountain between Biergarten and Sommerfest?

WE-15. What color is the teddy bear's nose in Der Teddybear's sign at Germany?

WE-16. What runs through the little village between Germany and Italy?

WE-17. Where will you find gondola poles?

WE-18. What animal is on the handles to the doors at La Gemma Elegante?

WE-19. What are the monks holding on the columns of La Gemma Elegante?

WE-20. What symbol is on the white portion of the crest above the Via Benvenuti shop sign?

WE-21.

AllEars® Mousy Mindboggler

Hickory Dickory Dock
The mouse who runs up this clock
Sure will be tired when he reaches the spire
He's bound to let out an "Ach!"

Hickory Dickory Dee
When it strikes it is something to see
Have you had too much beer? If you don't see it here
Then go back to the Old Country.

What and where is this?

Epcot's
World Showcase East

✠ ✠

WE-22. How many people could the Forbidden City Courtyards hold?

WE-23. When was the Cantina de San Angel founded?

WE-24. How many Stave churches exist today?

WE-25. In the Fontana di Nettuno, what does the god have in his hands?

WE-26. What is the brick pattern behind La Gemma Elegante?

WE-27. What does the clocktower in Germany do at the top of the hour?

WE-28. What color is the body of the airplane in Der Teddybear?

WE-29. What does the caribou mean to the Miao?

WE-30. What are the cliff divers holding on El Rio del Tiempo?

WE-31. How many trolls cast a spell on you on Maelstrom?

WE-32. The back of the Germany pavilion features a large landscape mural with red ribbon over it. What does the ribbon say?

WE-33. What hotel is at the end of El Rio del Tiempo?

WE-34. What kind of nuts can be found at the Outpost?

Epcot's
World Showcase East

✠ ✠

WE-35. Which four cultures are presented in "Land of Many Faces"?

WE-36. What marking is on the red-striped sail in Maelstrom's boarding area?

WE-37. What kind of box is hanging above the theater entrance at the end of Maelstrom?

WE-38. Why are wedding dresses red in Mongolia?

WE-39. Which three cruise lines have an office at the end of Maelstrom?

WE-40. How many acrobats are performing at the Peking Opera?

WE-41. What shape is the piñata the children are playing with in El Rio del Tiempo?

WE-42. What does every Naxi woman carry on her back?

WE-43. The Viking Ship Sports Stadium hosted what international sporting event in 1994?

WE-44. On which road did Marco Polo travel in the Gobi Desert?

WE-45. How many ballerinas appear in the movie at the end of Maelstrom?

WE-46. How many Yi live in China?

WE-47. How many polar bears are seen on Maelstrom?

Epcot's
World Showcase East
✠ ✠ ✠

WE-48. In what year was the Norway Showcase officially inaugurated?

WE-49. What kind of skis is the ski jumper wearing?

WE-50. What do dragons symbolize in reference to the emperors?

WE-51. Which Norwegian was the first to journey alone to the North Pole?

WE-52. What kind of scale is found above the Coca-Cola delivery truck at the Outpost?

WE-53. What is the name of the Naxi's slow, lilting, and haunting music?

WE-54. How many snowshoes are on display at The Puffin's Roost?

WE-55. How many dancers appear in the rainbow scene of El Rio del Tiempo?

WE-56. Which gondola poles are not paired?

WE-57. Who created the first rainwear in 1877?

WE-58. What department store can be seen in Reflections of China?

WE-59. What is Hitachi's logo?

WE-60. Where is the Fuente del Chorrito?

Epcot's
World Showcase East

✠ ✠ ✠

WE-61. How many stones are embedded in the floor of the Temple of Heaven?

WE-62. Who wrote the poem that was translated by Janet Gaston in the Stave Church?

WE-63. What's the ID number on the boat in "Norway—The Movie"? (Hint: It is seen in the harbor after you leave the Viking boat.)

WE-64. What color suits is the mariachi band wearing in the pool bar on El Rio del Tiempo?

WE-65. What city is between Tokyo and Lisbon at the Outpost's sign?

WE-66. How many armored figures appear above Das Kaufhaus?

WE-67. According to Reflections of China, the history of China has not only been written in ink, but what else?

WE-68. Where can you find the bell pictured below?

Epcot's
World Showcase West

✠

"The American Adventure is noble and bold, while Japan's culture is dignified and old. History of Morocco and France can enfold, and Canada and U.K.'s treasure is all gold."—Captain Skatt in his book, "The Folly of Fool's Gold: A Personal Account"

WW-1. What four countries have signs outside the Refreshment Port?

....

WW-2. How many totem poles are in or near the Canada pavilion?

....

WW-3. What is the skunk sitting on in the Trading Post in Canada?

....

WW-4. What character is depicted on the C button on the pressed penny machine in Canada?

....

WW-5. What is the motto of the Rose and Crown pub?

....

WW-6. In what year was the Yorkshire County Fish Shop established?

....

WW-7. How many soldiers are on the Toy Soldier shop sign?

....

WW-8. Where can you find a real bicycle at France? (Hint: It's not one of the bikes shown in the movie.)

....

WW-9. What Disney animated movie is reflected in a three-paned stained glass window in the France pavilion?

....

WW-10. What is the last phrase on the Les Chefs de France doors marked "Exit Only"?

....

WW-11. What color are Morocco's tiled roofs?

....

WW-12. What does "Bab" mean in Morocco?

....

Epcot's
World Showcase West

✠

WW-13. Now on display in Morocco, the Ghorrah water pitcher from the Batha Museum is what kind of terra cotta?

....

WW-14. What color are the rectangular glass panes on the doors to the Batha Museum in Morocco?

....

WW-15. What color is the big gate standing in front of the Japan pavilion?

....

WW-16. While standing in the Japanese garden, you may hear a rhythmic knocking sound. What makes this sound?

....

WW-17. How many samurai statues are on the castle's bridge in Japan?

....

WW-18. On the face of the clock at The American Adventure, what symbol represents 4?

....

WW-19. In what shop can you buy a copy of the Declaration of Independence?

....

WW-20.

AllEars® Mousy Mindboggler

You might want to eat them
But don't try with these!
Can't fry them or stew them
Though they're fresh from the seas.

In Epcot you'll find them
A treasure unmatched
When they're opened up
It's as though they've been hatched.

What is this?

....

Epcot's
World Showcase West

✠ ✠

WW-21. What is the address for Mr. Sanders?

WW-22. How many days did Thomas Jefferson say the founding fathers kept him in the loft while writing the Declaration of Independence in The American Adventure?

WW-23. According to the newspaper headline in The American Adventure, the police estimated that how many people showed up to greet Charles Lindbergh?

WW-24. How many Mounties on horseback in the "O Canada!" film?

WW-25. What is the address (number and street) of La Signature?

WW-26. How tall is the Goju-no-to pagoda at Japan?

WW-27. What is the name of the poem at the entrance to the Sportsman Shoppe?

WW-28. In what Canadian province is Butchart Gardens located?

WW-29. Burgundy is the world standard for what according to a sign in the France pavilion?

WW-30. How many kids are sliding down the luge in the film "O Canada!"?

WW-31. "Nanbutekki" is the Japanese word for what cooking pot?

WW-32. What was Mitsukoshi's first retail store name?

✠ ✠

WW-33. Robert Lillipid tin toys are believed to have originated when?

WW-34. What book is behind the cross and next to Notre Dame de Paris in Belle's Library at the France pavilion?

WW-35. Who is the photographer taking the picture of the family arguing over slavery in The American Adventure?

WW-36. In The American Adventure, how many feathers are in Chief Joseph's headdress?

WW-37. What is the most populated Canadian province?

WW-38. According Benjamin Franklin in The American Adventure, who never governs wisely?

WW-39. Where will you find a package addressed to A.A. Milne in the United Kingdom pavilion?

WW-40. What two items is the Spirit of Individualism statue holding in The American Adventure theater?

WW-41. How many doors are there to the CircleVision theater in Canada?

WW-42. What is the first statue to your right as you enter The American Adventure theater?

WW-43. Who makes a special appearance in The American Adventure?

Epcot's
World Showcase West

✠ ✠ ✠

WW-44. What number was Mary Lou Retton wearing in the film clip that appears in The American Adventure?

....

WW-45. What year was La Maison du Vin in the France pavilion established?

....

WW-46. At one point in the film "O Canada!," there is a Bulova clock. What is the temperature on the clock?

....

WW-47. What price is Aunt Louisa's London Toy Books "The London Alphabet" when mounted with linen?

....

WW-48. In what century did Japanese swords originate?

....

WW-49. What is the name on the helicopter in the Toy in Motion diorama in the Tin Toys museum?

....

WW-50. Scenes from what famous rodeo are found in the "O Canada!" film?

....

WW-51. According to the newsreel shown in The American Adventure, who is America's Air Ace?

....

Captain's Corner

Today I had the good fortune to view a documentary on the provincial experience. During the viewing, I spied my old chum, Capt. Eddie, whom I knew best as a race car driver. Others called him a "gallant ace," at least I think that's what they said. I understand Rickenbacker, as he was known to his war buddies, also flew biplanes in the War to End All Wars.

Epcot's
World Showcase West
✠ ✠ ✠

WW-52. Who wrote the quote that Ben Franklin recites in The American Adventure that Mark Twain doesn't remember writing?

WW-53. Who was leaving number 17 as the East wind blew?

WW-54. In The American Adventure show, what king signed the proclamation closing the Boston Harbor after the Boston Tea Party?

WW-55. In what city is the orginal Koutoubia Mosque minaret?

WW-56. Complete this sentence by Mark Twain: "I was born _____. Fortunately, it wore off."

WW-57. What newspaper's headline appears in The American Adventure proclaiming that Man Walks on the Moon?

WW-58. According to the two soldiers in The American Adventure, what did the English do while the Colonial army starved and froze at Valley Forge?

WW-59. What building is home to the movie "Impressions de France"?

WW-60. According to a scene in "O Canada!," what is available one block ahead, across from the museum?

WW-61. According to Will Rogers in The American Adventure, what does Congress want to fit in the bathtub?

Disney-MGM Studios'
Hollywood Boulevard

"Hooray for Hollywood, that thrilling, movieland Boulevard! Where any traveler, or young Indiana, can be romantic, with just a park-hopping pass! And any Movie Ride can be a Great Ride, when it shows fun unsurpassed! Come and try your luck, you could be Donald Duck. Hooray for Hollywood!"—Sung by Captain Skatt to the tune of "Hooray for Hollywood!" after too many fizzy drinks from the Hollywood Brown Derby

HB-1. What is Mickey Mouse standing on just inside the entrance to the park?

....

HB-2. How far is it to Anaheim according to Sid?

....

HB-3. What number train is on the Big Red Car billboard above Crossroads?

....

HB-4. What year did the Pacific Electric garage go up?

....

HB-5. What is the name of the Kodak-sponsored film shop?

....

HB-6. What number on Hollywood Blvd. is Pluto's Toy Palace?

....

HB-7. Who hosts the Starring Rolls Bakery?

....

HB-8. How many brooms from "Fantasia" appear in the grass outside the Brown Derby restaurant?

....

HB-9. What is the size of the big Sorcerer's Hat?

....

HB-10. Besides handprints, what other imprint did Alan Alda leave in the concrete in front of the Chinese Theater?

....

Disney-MGM Studios'
Hollywood Boulevard

✠ ✠

HB-11. How many black spaces are there on the holographic chess table in the queue of the Great Movie Ride?

....

HB-12. In what year was the original Hollywood Brown Derby established?

....

HB-13. On what date did Kermit leave his handprints in front of the Chinese theater?

....

HB-14. What two props from "Indiana Jones and the Temple of Doom" are found in the Great Movie Ride queue?

....

HB-15. According to the map in the restaurant lobby, what hotel is located across the street from the Wilshire Blvd. Brown Derby?

....

HB-16. On the Great Movie Ride, what color scarf is the munchkin wearing in the manhole at the beginning of the yellow brick road?

....

HB-17. The office of what company is located next to the L.A. Cinema Storage shop on Hollywood Blvd.?

....

HB-18. Who left their handprints beside Christy Brinkley's handprints at the Chinese theater?

....

HB-19. Who sponsors the first aid station?

....

HB-20. Did Steve Martin leave handprints or footprints in the concrete in front of the Chinese theater?

....

HB-21. What street corner is found by the marquee as you board the Great Movie Ride vehicles?

....

Disney-MGM Studios'
Hollywood Boulevard

✠ ✠

HB-22. What is the name of the school found behind Gene Kelly on the Great Movie Ride?

....

HB-23. What city is 7,034 miles away from the park?

....

HB-24. James Cagney is standing in front of what social club in the Great Movie Ride?

....

HB-25. According to the narrator on the Great Movie Ride, what character are you with onboard the Nostromo?

....

HB-26. What pier number is located next to the one-way tunnel at the end of the gangster scene in the Great Movie Ride?

....

HB-27. According to the marquee as you board the Great Movie Ride vehicles, what is the size of the cast?

....

HB-28.

AllEars® Mousy Mindboggler

Forgotten but not really gone,
I stand here by myself
If I could fit, I'm sure,
they would have put me on a shelf.

I'm not sure why I was replaced—
maybe I got a big head?
But surely my replacement
could be accused of that instead.

I'm still here if you miss me,
you can see me if you try
Back where they park their vehicles
and tram cars pass on by.

Who or what am I?

....

✠ ✠ ✠

HB-29. When won't Oscar fill your auto?

....

HB-30. What is the license plate number of the black car driven by the gangsters in the Great Movie Ride?

....

HB-31. How many miles of standard trolley lines does the Pacific Electric Railway have?

....

HB-32. How much does parking cost behind Adrian and Edith's?

....

HB-33. What kind of animal is found on the side porch of Sid's store?

....

HB-34. What is the finest property in Southern California?

....

HB-35. Who is the therapist at the Lend a Paw clinic?

....

HB-36. What is the name of the garden gnome in the side garden of Sid's store?

....

HB-37. Who is the Hollywood tailor?

....

HB-38. What two things are Pocahontas Remedies good for according to the ad in the Great Movie Ride?

....

HB-39. What is the phone number for Melrose?

....

HB-40. James Cagney is shown as a mobster in the underworld scene of the Great Movie Ride. What Irish bar is found in this scene?

....

HB-41. What does the sign by the telephones read in the Casablanca scene in the Great Movie Ride?

....

Disney-MGM Studios'
Sunset Boulevard

"Rock in a limo; ride the Tower up and down; see old Tinseltown."
—*A haiku by Captain Skatt*

SB-1. What color is Mickey's hat on the Mouse About Town store sign?

....

SB-2. Walt Disney is pictured in some photos at Mouse About Town. In those photos, what is he doing?

....

SB-3. What is trapped in amber in the Planet Hollywood Super Store?

....

SB-4. An image of what animal is found on top of Toluca Legs Turkey Co.?

....

SB-5. What is in the Carthay Circle Theater on Sunset Boulevard?

....

SB-6. What theatre hosts Beauty and the Beast?

....

SB-7. What color is the huge Stratocaster guitar?

....

SB-8. What is offered at the Rock Around the Shop at Rock n' Roller Coaster?

....

SB-9. What products are displayed above the dressing mirror in the Tower Gallery shop?

....

Disney-MGM Studios'
Sunset Boulevard

✠ ✠

SB-10. In what year was the Hollywood Tower Hotel established?

SB-11. At the Legends of Hollywood theater, how much is the featured movie matinee special?

SB-12. The first time your service elevator stops, there is a a sign for the hotel rooms that are located on that hallway. What room numbers are they?

SB-13. What number streetcar is found outside Sunset Ranch Market?

SB-14. What year was Sunset Hills Estates established?

SB-15. What street number on Sunset Boulevard is found between the Carthay Circle Theater and Mouse About Town?

SB-16. At what stand can you buy a pickle on Sunset Boulevard?

SB-17. Where can you "shop the world over" at the Hollywood Tower Hotel?

SB-18. What are the names of the three ballrooms at the exit of the Hollywood Tower Hotel?

SB-19. What state has its name on a guitar case in the Rock 'n' Roller Coaster gift shop?

SB-20. What ice company can be found behind the Sunset Club Couture shop?

SB-21. At the Tower of Terror, a mathematical equation appears several times. What is it?

Disney-MGM Studios'
Sunset Boulevard

✠ ✠

SB-22. What words are formed by the letters that have fallen to the bottom of the directory sign in the Hollywood Tower Hotel lobby?

SB-23. What is the record company featured in Rock 'n' Roller Coaster?

SB-24. What farm grows the potatoes for McDonald's french fries?

SB-25. What do you do with your hunger at Catalina Eddy's?

SB-26. According to the sign above Mouse About Town shop, "Lights, Camera, Breakfast with _____."

SB-27. Name at least one of the license plates on the super-stretch limos at Rock 'n' Roller Coaster.

SB-28. What is Rosie's Victory Garden slogan?

SB-29. What band recorded "Chicken Exit" at Rock 'n' Roller Coaster?

SB-30.

AllEars® Mousy Mindboggler

Even though I'm way stretched out
I never change my shape
In fact, folks says I'm super—
I have it on videotape!

If you should come to see me
I hope your stomach is strong
I might not make you walk this way
But I bet you'll sing along!

What am I, and where do you find me?

Disney-MGM Studios'
Sunset Boulevard
✠ ✠ ✠

SB-31. What is the number for Hollywood Realty?

SB-32. In the preshow film for the Twilight Zone Tower of Terror, what time is it on the clock behind the check-in desk?

SB-33. What's the sign of happy motoring?

SB-34. How did G-Force Records fall on hard times?

SB-35. What day was the world premier gala of Rock 'n' Roller Coaster?

SB-36. What was for dessert at the Hollywood Tower Hotel Sunset room on October 31, 1939?

SB-37. What is detective Nick Planet doing during Mystery in Hollywood?

SB-38. What initials are on the suitcase under the concierge desk of the Hollywood Tower Hotel?

SB-39. What do you do if you want to make a delivery to L.A. Cinema Storage?

SB-40. Director's Best Friend Inc. specializes in what?

SB-41. Who makes the police telegraph box on the side of the Carthay Circle Theater?

SB-42. What two Disney villians appear in both their forms in Sweet Spells?

SB-43. What is the home of the Victory Dog?

Disney-MGM Studios'
Echo Lake

✠

"Indiana, Drew, and Captain Rex—these heroes leave me perplexed. One dodges bullets, spears, and boulders, while another dodges meteors and Star Destoyers. The third hero leaves me in the dark wondering about his last remark."—Captain Skatt, journal entry

EL-1. What realtor is located at the intersection of Keystone and Echo Park?

EL-2. Which soft drink has a billboard above Hollywood and Vine?

EL-3. Walt was honored in which Annual Television Academy Hall of Fame?

EL-4. What's the name of the boat that houses the Dockside Diner?

EL-5. What star color does Minnesota get on the map in the back of the Adventure Outpost shop?

EL-6. What name is on Drew Carey's name badge on the Sounds Dangerous billboard?

EL-7. What will not work for calls from the pay phone in the phone booth on the left wall of Backlot Express?

EL-8. Star Tours is set on which stage?

EL-9. Where can you find the decoration shown below?

Disney-MGM Studio's
Echo Lake

✠ ✠

EL-10. When did Gertie the Dinosaur first amaze audiences?

EL-11. What street number is the building that houses the 50s Prime Time Cafe on Echo Park?

EL-12. According to the sign at the Indiana Jones stroller parking, what time is the crew due back?

EL-13. What phone extension would you dial to reach the Commissary from the Star Tours set?

EL-14. According to the sign above Hollywood and Vine, how much is daily rental of office space?

EL-15. What type of truck do you almost hit at the end of your Star Tours flight?

EL-16. Who is your captain on Star Tours?

EL-17. What island is on the stunt board in the back left corner of Backlot Express?

EL-18. What droid gets in trouble for talking to humanoids waiting to board a Star Tours shuttle?

EL-19. In 1984, who was first inducted into the Television Arts and Sciences Hall of Fame?

EL-20. From what film is the Dockside Diner?

EL-21. According to a sign in Backlot Express, "Material is _____, _____ _____."

EL-22. What type of bag does Drew Carey's character choose to have placed on his head in Sounds Dangerous?

Disney-MGM Studios'
Echo Lake

✠ ✠

EL-23. What should you not do to the excavation rope outside the Indiana Jones show theater entrance?

EL-24. What is prohibited at the time clock in Backlot Express?

EL-25. In the Cairo marketplace scene of the Indiana Jones show, there are two rolled-up canopies on the center building. What two colors are the upper canopy?

EL-26. What does the red tag dangling from the Star Tours captain say?

EL-27. What sector do you enter in the queue between the Star Tours work area with C3PO and R2-D2 and the boarding gates?

EL-28. Johnny Marscone, now the barber in Sounds Dangerous, was formerly known by what name?

EL-29. According to the information at Backlot Express, where did Walt Disney Pictures film "Country"?

EL-30. What circus act does Johnny send Drew Carey to see in Sounds Dangerous?

EL-31. How many statutes holding axes appear in the first scene of the Indiana Jones Stunt Spectacular?

EL-32. In the Star Tours pre-boarding instruction film, how many Ewoks board the Endor shuttle?

EL-33. What is the name of the show they are filming a pilot for in Sounds Dangerous?

Disney-MGM Studios'
Echo Lake

✠ ✠ ✠

EL-34. In what year was the building where Eddie Valiant has his office built?

....

EL-35. What flight number is the nonstop flight to Endor?

....

EL-36. What Star Tours flight do you actually take to the Endor Moon?

....

EL-37. What is the call number of the jeep with the mounted gun in the final scene of the Indiana Jones show?

....

EL-38. What is Star Tours departure frequency?

....

EL-39. When is the Walt Disney Imagineering holiday dinner?

....

EL-40. What county is Scarlet O'Hara from?

....

EL-41. What is the secret code for the art smuggling shipment in Sounds Dangerous?

....

EL-42. Who lives in apartment 106 in the Echo Lake Apartments?

....

EL-43. What is Ruth Payne's address?

....

EL-44. What is the address for Canbra Pines Lodge? (Hint: Check Backlot Express.)

....

EL-45. How many spears come out of the floor to try to skewer Indiana Jones in the stunt show?

....

EL-46. According to the boxes near the Dip Site, where are they shipping Prof. Henry Jones Jr.'s crate?

....

Disney-MGM Studios'
Streets of America

✠

"America, the melting pot, has many roads and ways—some from London, or China, and even the City by the Bay. The longest street of all celebrates great New York and from its pavement you can hear the echoes of loud torque."—Captain Skatt's journal, July 4

SA-1. What has crashed into the Sci-Fi Dine-In Theater sign?

SA-2. In the fountain in front of Muppet*Vision 3-D, what is Miss Piggy holding?

SA-3. What is Woody doing on the roof of Toy Story Pizza Planet?

SA-4. What color is the ringed planet in the Toy Story Pizza Planet logo?

SA-5. How many green men are hanging from the ceiling of Pizza Planet?

SA-6. What is the cow jumping over on top of the silo of Al's Toy Barn?

SA-7. What is hanging under the basket of the shopping cart at Al's Toy Barn?

SA-8. To what number is the dial pointing on the Lights, Motors, Action! Extreme Stunt Show sign?

SA-9. What is the speed limit on New York Street?

SA-10. MacDonald and Co. Brokers are located on the second floor of what New York Street address?

SA-11. What ginseng company can be found just off New York Street?

Disney-MGM Studios'
Streets of America

✠ ✠

SA-12. What funeral director is located at the corner of Gillespie Street?

SA-13. What Muppet Labs suite houses Kermit the Frog's office?

SA-14. What is on the third floor fire escape of the Brockerhoff?

SA-15. Gonzo tap dances during the Muppet*Vision 3-D preshow. What does he have on his head while he dances?

SA-16. Complete this sentence: "The Muppet Labs Division of Fashion Technology is 'Making Tommorow __ _____ _____ __ ___.'"

SA-17. Sal's Pawn Shop pays cash for what items?

SA-18. Why did the penguins take the Muppet orchestra job?

SA-19. What do you do in case of emergency in the Muppet store?

SA-20. Who is the director of the Muppet production "Two Bit Quarters"?

SA-21. Which one of the Three D's dancers in the Muppet*Vision 3-D preshow does not have a name that starts with "D"?

SA-22. Who does Rizzo Rat impersonate in the Muppet*Vision 3-D preshow?

SA-23. In the Muppet*Vision 3-D show, what does Fozzie's banana cream pie need?

Disney-MGM Studios'
Streets of America

✠ ✠

SA-24. What does Bean Bunny do in the Muppet*Vision 3-D's grand finale?

SA-25. How much is Rizzo Rat paid for his part in the preshow of Muppet*Vision 3-D?

SA-26. What is under the mat at the Muppet Theater box office?

SA-27. Who provides the estimated wait time at Muppet*Vision 3-D?

SA-28. Who works the projector in Muppet*Vision 3-D?

SA-29. How many boxes of Miss Piggy's satin gowns are in the Muppet*Vision preshow area?

SA-30. How many pulls does it take for Beaker to start the Muppet*Vision 3-D machine?

SA-31. What is written on the back of the Pizza Planet delivery shuttle?

SA-32.

AllEars® Mousy Mindboggler

It isn't easy being me
The guys I work with frustrate me
My best girl isn't very sweet
And worst of all I have webbed feet!

I'm in a land of movie stars
And sometimes they let me have a car
But mostly I am in a dimension
Sure to capture your attention

Who am I? And where can you find me?

Disney-MGM Studios'
Streets of America

✠ ✠ ✠

SA-33. Where is the Scientific Doohickey Company located?

SA-34. What type of team does Waldo plan to start after Beaker uses the Inflate-O-Matic on him in Muppet*Vision 3-D?

SA-35. What type of shop is located above Mama Melrose's?

SA-36. How much is the pearl bracelet in the window of Sal's Pawn Shop?

SA-37. What color jello is hanging from a net suspended from the ceiling?

SA-38. Where are "2-D Fruities"?

SA-39. Who paid for the billboard of the largest star of Muppet*Vision 3-D?

SA-40. Where is the sign pictured in the photo below?

Disney-MGM Studios'
Mickey Avenue

✠

"Greet Mickey Mouse the Big Cheese, then see the Little Mermaid ask for knees. The Backlot Tour shows simulated seas, and Big Bear and his friends are sure to please!"—Captain Skatt's letter to his niece and nephew before their first trip to Disney World

MA-1. How many stick figures are on the sign over the "Honey, I Shrunk the Kids" playground entrance?

MA-2. What eatery is the statue of Flik standing near?

MA-3. Where is the ACME ton of bricks?

MA-4. What mermaid bathes in a fountain outside the backstage tram tour?

MA-5. Who is the producer of "Mickey Mouse and You"?

MA-6. Over the entrance to the Voyage of the Little Mermaid are a sign and several characters from the show. Where is Flounder, the yellow fish?

MA-7. What sort of hat is Mickey Mouse wearing in the sign above the entrance to the Magic of Disney Animation?

MA-8. What soundstage houses Playhouse Disney?

MA-9. What is flying over the sign for Playhouse Disney?

Captain's Corner

I encountered one of the merpeople after a fall from my boat. She was blond and beautiful. I recall her name rhymed with Addison. She loves to frolic in bathtubs and fountains.

Disney-MGM Studios'
Mickey Avenue
✠ ✠

MA-10. In the model of Main Street, U.S.A. that is found in One Man's Dream, what is the name of the health food store?

MA-11. According to the display in One Man's Dream, how many stories tall is the Tree of Life?

MA-12. How many ounces does the giant water-spraying Coke bottle hold on Mickey Avenue?

MA-13. In what year did Walt's dad move his family to Marceline?

MA-14. Play-Doh is for what age group?

MA-15. According to a display in One Man's Dream, at which World's Fair did Walt Disney present Progressland?

MA-16. The "Honey, I Shrunk the Kids" playground has a giant Kodak film roll. What process speed is the film?

MA-17. What character appears first in the Voyage of the Little Mermaid show?

MA-18. During the Voyage of the Little Mermaid stage show, one of the main characters is blown away by the blowfish. Which character is it?

MA-19. How many swans are in the model of Disneyland's Sleeping Beauty Castle found in One Man's Dream?

MA-20. Whose pegleg hangs right inside the entrance to the Voyage of the Little Mermaid?

Disney-MGM Studios'
Mickey Avenue
✠ ✠

MA-21. What happens if you put your hand in the giant dog's nostril?

MA-22. What four colors are on the snail shells that can be seen in the Voyage of the Little Mermaid show?

MA-23. Who sings the "Goodbye Song" in Playhouse Disney?

MA-24. Who distributed Walt Disney's Alice comedies according to the sign in One Man's Dream?

MA-25. What color is the Play-Doh is in the "Honey, I Shrunk the Kids" playground?

MA-26. The Mickey Ave. sign was installed for what movie?

MA-27 According to the Voyage of the Little Mermaid stage show, how old is Ariel?

MA-28. How many shells are on the rock under Sebastian when he first appears in the Voyage of the Little Mermaid show?

MA-29. According to the film presentation in One Man's Dream, for how many years did Walt deliver papers?

MA-30. According to the film in One Man's Dream, Walt Disney's father worked as a carpenter at what building?

MA-31. Whose prison can be found right above the pegleg at the entrance to the Voyage of the Little Mermaid?

Disney-MGM Studios'
Mickey Avenue
✠ ✠ ✠

MA-32. Walt Disney was the editor of McKinley's smallest paper. What was its name?

....

MA-33. Steamboat Willie premiered at what theater?

....

MA-34. Gepetto's candle is seen in the preshow waiting area for the Voyage of the Little Mermaid. Where is it found?

....

MA-35. What famous celebrity wrote a letter to Walt saying, "I was greatly pleased to see your latest Silly Symphony, 'Who Killed Cock Robin?'"

....

MA-36. Where did Walt move after he was discharged from the ambulance corps?

....

MA-37. In the One Man's Dream film, in what year did Walt Disney admit to suffering "a heck of a breakdown"?

....

MA-38. The front page of what newspaper is shown declaring the beginning of World War II in One Man's Dream?

....

MA-39. In what year was Blain Gibson's sculpture of Abe Lincoln made?

....

MA-40. What type of suitcase did Walt Disney use for his trip to California?

....

MA-41. According to the film in One Man's Dream, what was the original budget for Mary Poppins?

....

Disney's Animal Kingdom's
Oasis and Discovery Island

✠

"An oasis of wild treasure awaits thee—discover the isle and its famous tree!"—Captain Skatt's journal, volume 365

DI-1. What restaurant is located at the park entrance?

DI-2. Garden Gate Gifts hosts a camera center sponsored by what company?

DI-3. What type of iguanas are displayed in the Oasis?

DI-4. As you cross the bridge from the Oasis to Discovery Island, what type of animal appears atop the two blue poles?

DI-5. What dam-building animal is prominently displayed over the Island Mercantile cash register farthest from the park entrance?

DI-6. What animal represents Australia on the globe at the Disney Vacation Club Information Center?

DI-7. The backs of the outdoor chairs at Pizzafari are shaped like what insect?

DI-8. What insect makes up the light poles outside the Baby Care Center?

DI-9. White-faced tree ducks don't quack. What noise do they make?

DI-10. Where can you find the birdhouses pictured to the right?

Disney's Animal Kingdom's
Oasis and Discovery Island
✠ ✠

DI-11. According to the sign in the Oasis, why is the swamp wallaby population decreasing?

....

DI-12. Fill in the blanks: "Please refrain from _____, _____, _____, or _____" during "It's Tough to be a Bug!"

....

DI-13. On the lights outside Beastly Bazaar, what animal can you see along with the snail?

....

DI-14. What type of weevil is Weevil Kneevil according to his poster in the lobby of the Tree of Life theater?

....

DI-15. What bird is the largest of all parrots?

....

DI-16. How many known species of spiders are there?

....

DI-17. What does "Babirusa" mean?

....

DI-18. How many bugs a day can the southern giant anteater eat?

....

DI-19. In the "Its Tough to Be a Bug!" lobby is a poster for "The Grass Menagerie." What does the sign the bug is holding say?

....

DI-20. What type of spoonbill shares a display with the scarlet ibis at the entrance to the park?

....

DI-21. What's the name of the bug spray in "It's Tough to Be a Bug!"?

....

DI-22. What two kinds of lemurs are found behind the "It's Tough to Be a Bug!" FASTPASS distribution area?

....

Disney's Animal Kingdom's
Oasis and Discovery Island
✠ ✠

DI-23. What type of place to shop and eat is the Rainforest Cafe?

....

DI-24. What insects act as spotlights for "It's Tough to Be a Bug!"?

....

DI-25. A Disney Princess from what film is featured in the central display of Creature Comforts?

....

DI-26. What is the hit song from "The Dung and I"?

....

DI-27. What animal is not a display case in Creature Comforts: a gorilla, a zebra, or a giraffe?

....

DI-28. What type of duo is the Dung Brothers?

....

DI-29. What type of animal is found at the very top of the Flame Tree Barbeque sign?

....

DI-30. According to the poster in "It's Tough to Be a Bug!," how many flowers must honeybees visit to gather enough nectar for one teaspoon of honey?

....

DI-31. How many boards make up the suspension bridge in the Oasis?

....

DI-32. What animal is shown on the lights over the central register of Island Mercantile?

....

DI-33. What theatre company performs in the Tree of Life theater?

....

DI-34. What animals are blending into the blue Pizzafari Pizza sign?

....

Disney's Animal Kingdom's
Oasis and Discovery Island
✠ ✠ ✠

DI-35. Who is the reporter for the Holly Wood Reporter?

DI-36. What animal has the scientific name Axis axis?

DI-37. Unlike most other ducks, what does a male wigeon do?

DI-38. How many ladybugs can protect one acre of crops?

DI-39. What is the Indian spotbill duck named for?

DI-40. What do blue and yellow macaws chew on for a mineral source?

DI-41. What is the critical review of "A Stinkbug Named Desire" and who made the review?

DI-42. What is the scientific name of the black swan?

DI-43. Ruddy ducks have what color bills?

DI-44. How much does the giant galapagos tortoise weigh?

Captain's Corner

I have stumbled upon a remarkable treasure grove upon leaving the Insecta Pageant. The grove is inhabited by a Geochelone Elephantopus made famous by Mr. Darwin's Archipelago. Extraordinary discovery.

Note to self: Turn left.

Disney's Animal Kingdom's
Camp Minnie-Mickey

✠

"Hike the forests of the Adriondacks to meet animals that leave few tracks; from a lion that sings to a duck with no wings. Bring your autograph book as you wander these trails, for you're sure to meet princesses plus mice without tails."—Captain Skatt's article on remarkable animal physiology ("The Voyage of the Rodent")

MM-1. Where will you find a totem pole with a shark on it?

....

MM-2. How many character greeting trails are there?

....

MM-3. Shows found in Camp Minnie-Mickey are based on what two Disney films?

....

MM-4. What region does Camp Minnie-Mickey evoke?

....

MM-5. What color is Goofy's lunchbox?

....

MM-6. How many theaters are in Camp Minnie-Mickey?

....

MM-7. What did Donald catch while fishing?

....

MM-8. What is the shape of the Festival of the Lion King theater?

....

MM-9. Where will you find the fish pictured below?

....

Disney's Animal Kingdom's
Camp Minnie-Mickey
✠✠ & ✠✠✠

MM-10. How many named seating areas are there in Festival of the Lion King, and what are they called?

MM-11. What three characters from "The Lion King" movie appear in Festival of the Lion King?

MM-12. What duck is hiking with Huey, Dewey, and Louie?

MM-13. Which animal's float features a "waterfall" in Festival of the Lion King?

MM-14. What is the name of the large tree in Pocahontas and Her Forest Friends?

MM-15. Where does the Forest Trail lead?

MM-16. What's unusual about the birdhouses in Camp Minnie-Mickey?

MM-17. What are the "Tumble Monkeys"?

MM-18. Where can you see the "rock dragon"?

MM-19.

AllEars® Mousy Mindboggler
I am in two different spots
Within the same theme park
In one I stand in daylight
In the other, in the dark.
In both of my locations
I'm with creatures great and small
When you hear my gentle voice
You know I'm nature's call.

Who am I? And can you name my two locations?

Disney's Animal Kingdom's
Africa and Rafiki's Planet Watch

✠

"The Dark Continent awaits your explorations. To travel here you need no vaccinations." —Captain Skatt's safari journal

AF-1. What is the name of the village here in Africa?

AF-2. In what year was the village's fort erected?

AF-3. Based on a sign near the Dawa Bar, what must you do before returning to the guest house?

AF-4. According to the outside hanging sign, what kind of food does Tusker House have?

AF-5. What shop is the "last film" stop before the Kilimanjaro Safaris?

AF-6. Where in Tusker House will you find a detailed map of Harambe Wildlife Reserve?

AF-7. When does the Samburu Riding Safari depart?

AF-8. In what year was the Mkubwa House restored?

AF-9. What did Captain Bob invent?

AF-10. What train travels to Rafiki's Planet Watch?

Captain's Corner

Ah, the wonders of Africa. I lost my favorite teapot on a camping safari in the wilds of this dark continent. Captain Robert "Bob" Ongala checked all the tents in the event of any hanky panky, but he found only a set of drums. I miss that teapot dreadfully.

Disney's Animal Kingdom's
Africa and Rafiki's Planet Watch

✠ ✠

AF-11. Where will you find the good ship "Kiwandeo"?

AF-12. "Think __ times before you dabble in poaching."

AF-13. What is the "Kisiwa"?

AF-14. How many female Okapi clipboards are on the notes board on the Pangani Forest Exploration Trail?

AF-15. Who is the proprietor of Muziki?

AF-16. What two animal skulls can be found just past the exit of the Pangani Trail aviary?

AF-17 According to the meerkat notes on Pangani Trail, what response seems to be built-in?

AF-18. Based on the sign at the Dawa Bar, guests of the hotel are advised to not do what after dark?

AF-19. As shown in a display on the Pangani Trail, what is the estimated hippo population in East Africa?

AF-20. How many dominant males live in each group of Colobus monkeys?

AF-21. How old can baobob trees be?

AF-22. What is a hippo's main food?

AF-23. The Okapi is related to what other animal?

AF-24. What animal is the emblem of Harambe Wildlife Preserve?

Disney's Animal Kingdom's
Africa and Rafiki's Planet Watch

✠ ✠

AF-25. What are known as the "ghosts of the forest"?

AF-26. What is Peter's assignment in Tusker House?

AF-27. What kind of evil is animal poaching?

AF-28. What kind of tank is strapped to the back right of the safari trucks?

AF-29. What warden post is shown on the map as you enter Pagani Trail?

AF-30. What's the number one rule of behavior on the safari?

AF-31. Where is the Florida Panther National Wildlife Refuge located?

AF-32. Who is restoring Mombasa Marketplace?

AF-33. What animal is in the study burrow in the Pagani Trail Research Center?

AF-34. Who sent Dr. Kulunda the thank-you note that is posted at the exit of the Pagani Trail aviary?

AF-35. Who wrote "Natives and Strangers" in the library's collection of the Pagani Research Center?

AF-36. Why shouldn't you feed the baboons at Tusker House?

AF-37. What does "duma" mean?

Disney's Animal Kingdom's
Africa and Rafiki's Planet Watch

✠ ✠ ✠

AF-38. Catherine Johnson has what kind of degree?

AF-39. How much are the electric torches/Kurunzi at Ziwani Traders?

AF-40. What color is the stripe on the canteen at the Kilimanjaro Safaris' poachers' camp?

AF-41. What is the phone number of Zidia Charities?

AF-42. To whom can complaints be addressed at the train station?

AF-43. According to the box in the Pangani Trail gorilla area, where was the confiscated poacher gear sent?

AF-44. What is the post office box and telephone number for Ziwani Traders?

AF-45. What railroad has a bridge seen while on Kilimanjaro Safaris?

AF-46. Who did Darla finally mate with: Charlie, Kail, or Carlos? *It sure wasn't me! — Jack*

AF-47. According to the sign on Kiliminjaro Safaris, what may go away during rainy season?

AF-48. Translate this phrase: "Upishi Umekatazwa."

AF-49. Why is there no admittance to the beach at Harambe Port?

AF-50. What does the giant African bullfrog eat?

Disney's Animal Kingdom's
Asia

✠

"Down the white river, up the highest mountain peak, the tigers beckon."—Haiku by Captain Skatt in honor of Expedition: Everest

AS-1. How many spires adorn the bridge as you enter Asia from Discovery Island?

AS-2. What animal appears on the Drinkwallah sign?

AS-3. What stage hosts Flights of Wonder?

AS-4. What pair of animals graces the bronze bell near the Chakranadi Chicken Shop?

AS-5. Complete this name: "Anandapur _____ Forest."

AS-6. What type of adventure is Kali River Rapids?

AS-7. How many elephants squirt at rafts at the end of Kali River Rapids?

AS-8. Upon what river is Kali River Rapids?

AS-9. When does the hotel on the path between DinoLand U.S.A. and Asia open?

AS-10. What is wrong with the tire on the decorated blue truck?

AS-11. Where can you find the gong pictured to the right?

Disney's Animal Kingdom's
Asia

✠ ✠

AS-12. When was the royal forest given to the people of Anandapur?

....

AS-13. On the path between DinoLand U.S.A. and Asia, how many kilograms does the small propane tank outside Gupta's Gear weigh?

....

AS-14. What is the "So Sari"?

....

AS-15. Besides a Trekkers Inn, what else is at Shangri La on the path between Asia and DinoLand U.S.A.?

....

AS-16. Who sponsors the Kodak picture spot near Mandala Gifts in Asia?

....

AS-17. According to the sign, what phone company operates the telephones at the restrooms between Asia and DinoLand U.S.A.?

....

AS-18. A picture of what mountain range is found inside Drinkwallah?

....

AS-19. What handheld musical instrument hangs from the ceiling in the first building of the Kali River Rapids queue?

....

AS-20. What sea is south of the Kingdom of Anandapur?

....

AS-21. On what river is the Kataka Tiger Camp?

....

AS-22. What is the bathing load at the fountains near Maharajah Jungle Trek?

....

AS-23. As you enter the queue for Kali River Rapids, what is written on the side of the large crate?

....

Disney's Animal Kingdom's
Asia

✠ ✠

AS-24. In the Kali River Rapids queue, what currency gets better prices at the shop?

....

AS-25. The Kali River Rapids queue has several Buddhist statues in the grass. How many statues still have heads?

....

AS-26. Who owns the shop found in the Kali River Rapids queue?

....

AS-27. According to the Anadapur Regional Irrigation District marker on the path between DinoLand U.S.A. and Asia, what station number is at the marker?

....

AS-28. According to the calendar in the bat house, what day is Feast Day?

....

AS-29. What must be worn at all times while rafting on Kali River Rapids?

....

AS-30. What is the name of the shop selling McDonald's french fries?

....

AS-31. What type of aerial acrobatics can be seen at Flights of Wonder?

....

AS-32. What programme placed the electric and telephone poles near the exit of Kali River Rapids, according to the sign on each pole?

....

AS-33. How many pitchers are under the Safe Water for Travelers water fountain on Maharajah Jungle Trek?

....

AS-34. Where is the komodo dragon's natural habitat?

....

Disney's Animal Kingdom's
Asia

✠ ✠ ✠

AS-35. What day of the week is the Sanjit wedding?

....

AS-36. How many statues are at the top of the Kali River Rapids lift hill?

....

AS-37. What air transport company has a sign next to Mandala Gifts?

....

AS-38. How many meters tall is Mount Machapuchre?

....

AS-39. Bats can eat up to how many insects an hour?

....

AS-40. What logging company's truck is found on Kali River Rapids?

....

AS-41. Who painted the sign for Gupta's Gear?

....

AS-42. What is the phone number of the Leopard Lodge?

....

AS-43. Eki's Hotel has what in most rooms?

....

AS-44. What Kali River raft was due back yesterday?

....

AS-45. How many stories are told in the painted ceilings just before you enter the shop in the Kali River Rapids queue?

....

AS-46. What type of animals are frequently encountered in the ruins ahead on the Maharajah Jungle Trek?

....

AS-47. Who is the proprieter of Kali River Expeditions?

....

AS-48. Who will see Roshana at her handy drink stand in the spring?

....

Disney's Animal Kingdom's
DinoLand U.S.A.

✠

"Chester and Hester greet you oddly; dinos roam this land so proudly!"—Captain Skatt's journal entry on the day of The Dig

DL-1. What is the name of the bridge at the entrance?

DL-2. What is the speed limit on U.S. 498?

DL-3. How many riders can fit in one Primeval Whirl time machine?

DL-4. In what county is Chester and Hester's?

DL-5. What can be found hanging from the ceiling of the auto repair area of Restaurantosaurus?

DL-6. Who made the jukebox in Restaurantosaurus' Hip Joint?

DL-7. In what year was The Boneyard established?

DL-8. How many spill chutes exit from the T-Rex hill in The Boneyard?

DL-9. In the fossil recovery list on the T-Rex hill, what is the common name for the Beauticus Shartara line?

DL-10.

AllEars® Mousy Mindboggler
In a land that's full of critters
You might think I'm just another
But I'm really very rare—like me there is no other
Well, OK, I'm just a replica
Chicago's my real home
So sue me—call me a copy
Sticks and stones won't break my bones.

Who am I? And where will you find me?

Disney's Animal Kingdom's
DinoLand U.S.A.

✠ ✠

DL-11. When did the Columbian Mammoth found across the Oldengate bridge from The Boneyard perish?

DL-12. Who has the favored assumptions on the fossil matrix sign in The Boneyard?

DL-13. According to the plaque in the Hip Joint of Restaurantosaurus, in what year did Nighel Smith win the Bonehead Award?

DL-14. What color is the broach on Dr. Marsh's blouse in the Dinosaur preshow?

DL-15. Restaurantosaurus has a Pterodactyl _____. Spelling counts!

DL-16. Who painted Mesozoic Dawn at Restaurantosaurus?

DL-17. According to the display in The Boneyard, what is the length of the Hadrosauridae?

DL-18. The hitchhiking dinos on Primeval Whirl are heading for the ____ ____ or bust.

DL-19. If you want the broken pay phone inside Chester & Hester's store repaired, what number would you call?

DL-20. The future is what according to Dr. Marsh?

DL-21. "Dying of thirst" is the slogan for what drink advertised in Restaurantosaurus?

DL-22. In the Dino Institute, what color writing is on the Flux Ducts?

Disney's Animal Kingdom's
DinoLand U.S.A.

✠ ✠

DL-23. What time is The Boneyard site geology lecture?

DL-24. What time is it on the clock on the back of the Primeval Whirl time machines?

DL-25. How many dino dig sites are shown on the map at the Disney Vacation Club kiosk?

DL-26. As you walk up the ramp to board Primeval Whirl, there is a long time machine between the two boarding areas. How many scientists operate it?

DL-27. In case of Emergency of Excessive Heat in Restaurantosaurus, what should one do?

DL-28. At what Cretaceous Trail dig site location can you find the Hadrosaur being plastered?

DL-29. What kind of transfer unit is in the back of a Dinosaur Time Rover?

DL-30. According to the signs at the end of Primeval Whirl, how long does it take to go from the past back to the present?

DL-31. What Boneyard scientist did the draft of Dig Site A42?

DL-32. How much is parking at Chester & Hester's?

DL-33. According to the sticker on the cooler on the roof above Restaurantosaurus' entrance, what animal is loved?

DL-34. What color is the bird in the cuckoo clock on the Primeval Whirl lift hill?

Disney's Animal Kingdom's
DinoLand U.S.A.

✠ ✠ ✠

DL-35. Complete this sentence: "Nothing is _____ about Chester & Hester's Dino-Rama."

DL-36. In the fossil room of Restaurantosaurus, what dinosaur rules?

DL-37. What year is BT's pet rock from?

DL-38. How much is premium gas at the Gilbarco Calco-Meter pump at Chester & Hester's?

DL-39. According to the signs outside of The Boneyard, what lost its tail?

DL-40. What Primeval Whirl time machine time setting is farther back in time than "way back in time"?

DL-41. What London hotel has a sticker on the Disney Vacation Club suitcases?

DL-42. Rex's Towing is King of what?

DL-43. What was the postage value of individual "The World of Dinosaur" stamps issued by the U.S. Postal Service?

DL-44. What did male Pachycephalosauruses ram together according to the sign in The Boneyard?

DL-45. A Deinocherus claw is a 75-million-year-old what?

DL-46. What's the number for Dino Dan's Dino Repair?

DL-47. What day is the Frisbee tournament between professors and students?

Downtown Disney's
Marketplace
✠

*"I visited these cafes and stores until I could simply walk no more.
I sat and sat and nursed my sores. Maybe I could just stay here
and play, earning a living with a Fish Cafe?"—Captain Skatt*

MP-1. What are the ten lions doing on the tenth day of Christmas at Disney's Days of Christmas Store?

....

MP-2. Six ducks are playing on the sixth day of Christmas. Where in the Christmas store are they?

....

MP-3. Who is playing basketball with Tigger in the middle of Team Disney?

....

MP-4. The windmill between Earl of Sandwich and Once Upon a Toy is made up of what kind of toys?

....

MP-5. Who is trying to "lasso" Mr Potato head in Once Upon a Toy?

....

MP-6. What park icon makes up the arrow on the giant "Life" game wheel?

....

MP-7. What character can be found on the very top spire of World of Disney?

....

MP-8. Whose hands hold up your clothes in the World of Disney fitting rooms?

....

MP-9. In the Alice room of World of Disney, what suit are the cards at the register?

....

MP-10. What does the long bumper sticker on the Lego alien spaceship read?

....

MP-11. What's the maximum time on the parking meters at the Lego Store?

....

MP-12. Where's the lantern on the right?

....

Downtown Disney's
Marketplace

✠ ✠ & ✠ ✠ ✠

MP-13. When did Domingo Ghirardelli live?

MP-14. Where are the four chiming bells for the fourth day of Christmas?

MP-15. Which edition of the the Twilight Bark Gazette announces that "Pongo Catches Crook, Rescues Puppies"?

MP-16. Who is grinning at the doors to the Alice room in World of Disney?

MP-17. Which Disney character can be found dressed as the Statue of Liberty?

MP-18. Other than a magic carpet, the Fab Four can be found traveling the world riding in what vehicle in World of Disney?

MP-19. What is Pluto balancing on his nose on the Team Mickey sign?

MP-20. Where are seven dwarfs mining?

MP-21. What's the name of the lady in the tree at Rainforest Cafe?

MP-22. What are the eleven puppies doing?

MP-23. What's Cap'n Jack holding on his sign?

Captain's Corner

My little cafe venture has been a success! I now know that the accordian was a better choice than tuba, which scares my lobsters.

Downtown Disney's
Pleasure Island

✠

"Old Merriweather Pleasure left us a legacy—I love the Club more than the high seas."—Captain Skatt after a late night

PI-1. What is the larger-than-life figure of Jessica Rabbit doing?

....

PI-2. What year was the "old" Pleasure Island founded?

....

PI-3. How old do you have to be to enter Mannequin's Dance Palace?

....

PI-4. What sort of fish adorns the Rock 'n' Roll Beach Club sign?

....

PI-5. How many stars are on the Reel Finds building?

....

PI-6. On what street is 8Trax?

....

PI-7. What's draped over the top of Adventurers Club?

....

PI-8. What club is holding an Open House?

....

PI-9. Where is the huge set of wind-up teeth?

....

PI-10. What is the name of the improv company that plays at the Comedy Warehouse?

....

PI-11.

AllEars® Mousy Mindboggler

Would you, could you see a show
Where they make it up as they go?
Could you, would you pay more bucks
If you were sure of lots of yucks?
This place is fun most definitely
To miss it is a tragedy.

What and where is this?

....

Downtown Disney's
Pleasure Island
✠ ✠ & ✠ ✠ ✠

PI-12. Which two letters appear under the "Waterfront" sign on the buoy at the exit of Comedy Warehouse?

PI-13. What year was Pleasure Island electrified?

PI-14. What businesses were housed in the Mannequin's building in the earlier part of the 20th century?

PI-15. What was Mrs. Pleasure's first name?

PI-16. What exact date is it perpetually inside the Adventurers Club?

PI-17. What's the price per gallon of Esso gas at Pleasure Island?

PI-18. What's the motto of Plankton's Seaside Yacht Repairs?

PI-19. When was Tony's Marine business established?

PI-20. When did the old Administration Building burn to the ground?

PI-21. What shop was responsible for stuffing the head of the rare Mongolian Yakoose?

PI-22. What was Merriweather Pleasure's middle name?

PI-23. How many people are sitting in the painting on the right side of the Library stage?

PI-24. What does Arnie the Comedy Mask wear in his hair?

Downtown Disney's
West Side

✠

"The West Side story is food and play—with shops to visit and Cirque du Soleil."—Captain Skatt's journal on a very humdrum day

WS-1. What is the name of the boat to the left of the Planet Hollywood entrance?

WS-2. What color is the awning above Mickey's Groove?

WS-3. What color is the superhero's mask on the Starabilias sign?

WS-4. What does the witch have in her hand on the Candy Cauldron sign?

WS-5. Where in Candy Cauldrion is a painting of a basket of apples in a castle?

WS-6. What is the motto of Wolfgang Puck's eateries?

WS-7. What shape is the "Q" in the DisneyQuest logo?

WS-8. What store is "On Location"?

WS-9. What color are the giant pineapple leaves at Bongo's Cuban Cafe?

WS-10. How many House of Blues signs are on the water tower?

WS-11. What does the Cirque du Soleil building resemble?

WS-12. Complete this sentence: "In _____ We Trust."

Downtown Disney's
West Side
✠ ✠ & ✠ ✠ ✠

WS-13. How do you avoid bad karma at the House of Blues?

WS-14. What's the name of the cafe at the Virgin Megastore?

WS-15. What color is the filmstrip on the automated box office sign?

WS-16. How many large, dark gray squares are in the center plaza pavement of West Side?

WS-17. What famous escape was a major highlight of Houdini's show from 1913 to 1926?

WS-18. What's the address of ABC's BBQ?

WS-19. How many bars does Bongo's have?

WS-20. What magician causes "a real live ponderous elephant" to instantly vanish?

WS-21. What's the home of Cream of Wheat cereal?

WS-22. Where can you find door handles in the shape of lightning bolts?

WS-23. Where will you find black leather chairs with a gold, stylized "S" on them?

WS-24. Where will you find the sign pictured on the right?

Resorts
All-Stars

"Disney's resort hotels are full of details—with so much to see you'll have plenty of tales!"—Captain Skatt's letter home to his niece and nephew

AR-1. How many lights hang down over the lobby concierge desk at All-Star Music?

....

AR-2. How many sailors are in the mural in All-Star Music's food court?

....

AR-3. What hockey team is depicted in the large mural at the End Zone Food Court?

....

AR-4. Who's pitching in the Grand Slam Pool?

....

AR-5. What number is Herbie the Lovebug?

....

AR-6. What's the decor of the staircases on the 101 Dalmatians buildings?

....

AR-7. Where at All-Star Sports will you find what's pictured in photo AR-7 below?

....

AR-8. Where at All-Star Movies will you find what's pictured in photo AR-8 below?

....

AR-9. Where at All-Star Music will you find what's pictured in photo AR-9 below?

....

AR-7

AR-8

AR-9

Resorts
All-Stars
✠ ✠ & ✠ ✠ ✠

AR-10. What color is Perdy's collar?

AR-11. On what street corner is Beauty and the Beast located?

AR-12. How many X's are on the football field?

AR-13. What's the bathing load of the Piano Pool?

AR-14. How many books are on Lucky's TV?

AR-15. What is Ariel holding at the Piano pool?

AR-16. In which starring role is Mickey presented at the Fantasia Pool?

AR-17. What number is found on all of the bats at the Home Run Hotel?

AR-18. How many toy soldiers are in the Bucket o' Soldiers?

AR-19. From what movie are the characters shooting water in the middle of the Calypso pool?

AR-20. What four team banners fly between the goal line and the 10-yard line nearest the food court?

AS-21. Which band plays the giant drum set in front of the Jazz Inn area?

AR-22. How many Spalding basketballs are on the two Hoops Hotel buildings?

Resorts
Animal Kingdom Lodge

✠

AK-1. What does "Karibuni" mean?

....

AK-2. What are the names of the two firepits?

....

AK-3. How many giraffes are in the mural in The Mara?

....

AK-4. What is the name of the arcade?

....

AK-5. What is the maximum occupancy of The Mara?

....

AK-6. What is the full name of the pool bar?

....

AK-7. On what trail is the fitness center located?

....

AK-8. What are the hours of the Zahanati fitness center?

....

AK-9. How tall is a giraffe at birth?

....

AK-10. What is another name for Ankole Cattle?

....

AK-11. What diamond award did AAA present to Jiko in 2003?

....

AK-12. The ladder just inside the entrance to the Arusha savanna was made by what people?

....

AK-13. From what do flamingos get their pink coloring?

....

From watching humans go skinny-dipping? — Jack

Resorts
Animal Kingdom Lodge
✠ ✠ & ✠ ✠ ✠

AK-14. From where are the Asante people?

AK-15. What does "Jiko" mean?

AK-16. Children under what age must have supervision at the Hakuna Matata playground?

AK-17. What animal lets its body temperature rise seven degrees higher than normal on very hot days?

AK-18. What are the hours of Simba's Cubhouse?

AK-19. What is the extension of the house phone in the guest laundry by Simba's Cubhouse?

AK-20. A map of what continent is on the floor, just inside the resort's lobby entry?

AK-21. What is the address of Animal Kingdom Lodge?

AK-22. Who made the Thornwood Canoe Carving?

AK-23. What is the maximum occupancy of Zahanati Fitness Center?

AK-24. Who wrote "I Married Adventure"?

AK-25. What plant's sharp thorns keep all but the hardiest or hungriest animals from stripping its leaves bare?

AK-26. How many square miles is Pennsylvania?

Resorts
BoardWalk

✠

BW-1. Hue G. Krazont is the proprietor of what?

....

BW-2. Who is the proprietor of Thimbles and Threads?

....

BW-3. Who is the fortune teller at the BoardWalk?

....

BW-4. What is the name of the boat dock?

....

BW-5. How many elephants are by the Luna Park pool?

....

BW-6. How many circular windows are under the
Dance Hall sign?

....

BW-7. Complete this: "Eat here tonite, Culinary
adventure, great food from the Mediterranean, Tapas
_____, Festive Restaurant."

....

BW-8.

AllEars® Mousy Mindboggler

My happy face creeps some folks out
I fill them full of dread
But they'd get over that if they would
Get inside my head.

To get a close-up look at me
You'd best be sitting down
See? I'm really smiling
There's no trace of a frown.

Don't look for ME inside though
That would be lunacy
Just walk outside -- I'm in the midst
Of fun frivolity.

What and where is this?

....

Resorts
BoardWalk
✠ ✠ & ✠ ✠ ✠

BW-9. How long has Dundy's Sundries been serving the BoardWalk?

....

BW-10. What is unusual about the horses in the lobby chandelier?

....

BW-11. Complete this sentence: Showplace of the

_____.

....

BW-12. What's the motto of Muscles and Bustles?

....

BW-13. There is a vehicle access road behind the BoardWalk along the canal. What is the speed limit?

....

BW-14. What color dress is Miss Florida wearing in Seaside Sweets?

....

BW-15. What two Garden Cottage suites share a gate/patio area?

....

BW-16. According to the picture outside the elevators by the fitness center, what is Puck's Hint to Hotel Keepers?

....

BW-17. How much is it to buy a ticket to ride the roller coaster in the lobby?

....

BW-18. Bertha, who is vacationing at Atlantic City, sent a postcard to Bess. Where does Bess live?

....

BW-19. How much does it cost to have Mystic Ray send you a message?

....

BW-20. In what three places of the U.S. is hot dog consumption the greatest?

....

Resorts
Caribbean Beach

✠

CB-1. How many people are in the painting across from the Bell Services desk?

....

CB-2. What color is the roof of the Customs House?

....

CB-3. What theme park can you see from the Promenade between Martinique and Old Port Royale?

....

CB-4. What is the name of the arcade?

....

CB-5. What is the name of the deli?

....

CB-6. How many bus stops are at this resort?

....

CB-7. What is the name of the marina?

....

CB-8. What is the depth of the pool where the slide enters the water?

....

CB-9. What is the bathing load of the Old Port Royale Pool?

....

CB-10. How many spitting lion heads are under the big waterfall at the theme pool?

....

Captain's Corner

This morning I explored Barefoot Bay, which is ringed with white sand beaches. The roofs of the natives' huts shine in the sun and present a remarkable picture. The scenery, if I may use such an expression, appeared to the sight harmonious. The good folks at Barefoot Bay Boatyard gave me the use of a boat for a slight sum. I passed by the watering hole, where I spied two lions.

Resorts
Caribbean Beach
✠ ✠ & ✠ ✠ ✠

CB-11. How many cannons are found at the Old Port Royale Pool?

CB-12. What characters appear on the chalkboards on the lifeguard stands at the Old Port Royale pool?

CB-13. Children under what age must have adult supervision at the kiddie pool?

CB-14. How many island beaches have playgrounds?

CB-15. What fruit is found above the ATM in Old Port Royale?

CB-16. What is the influence on the cuisine at Shutters?

CB-17. What color is the mailbox next to the Market Street Menu and Royale Pizza?

CB-18. What is the Banana Cabana?

CB-19. What is in a Goombay Smash?

CB-20. When is mail picked up at the Customs House?

CB-21. What is the fortune of wishes past?

CB-22. How many flags are there at the entrance circle to Old Port Royale?

CB-23. Where will you find this school of fish?

Resorts
Contemporary
✠

CO-1. There are two paintings in the lobby by the restrooms. Who's the artist?

....

CO-2. What are the hours of operation at the Food and Fun Center's Redemption Center?

....

CO-3. How many brooms surround the Mickey statue in the Fantasia shop?

....

CO-4. What is the bathing load (maximum capacity) for the main pool?

....

CO-5. Jiminy Cricket wants you to do what by the pool at the Contemporary?

....

CO-6. What two Disney characters are on the Contemporary Recreation chalkboard signs by the pool?

....

CO-7. What is Mickey holding on the fitness center sign?

....

CO-8.
AllEars® Mousy Mindboggler
Every night I make the rounds
But I am not on theme park grounds.

I shine so bright, I play a tune
And then I go dark all too soon.

What am I and where do you see me?

....

Contemporary
✠ ✠ & ✠ ✠ ✠

CO-9. What are the requirements to operate a Sea Raycer?

....

CO-10. What time is the final collection at the FedEx box in the convention center?

....

CO-11. Who conducted Paul Dukas' The Sorcerer's Apprentice in 1940?

....

CO-12. What number do you touch on a resort room phone to call recreation?

....

CO-13. What are the winter hours at Sammy Duvall?

....

CO-14. Chef Mickey is holding what two utensils?

....

CO-15. Where is the Butterfly House?

....

CO-16. Who is sitting on a pair of see-through Mickey ears?

....

CO-17. Where does the blue flag launch go?

....

CO-18. Whose hand is hanging from the ceiling and pointing to the restrooms at Chef Mickey's?

....

CO-19. What color is the five-legged goat on the mural?

....

CO-20. What year was Richard Baker born according to his artwork on the third floor?

....

CO-21. What does a vertical stripe of red and blue on a semaphore flag mean?

....

Resorts
Coronado Springs

✠

CS-1. What color are the poles that support the roof over the lobby's main drop-off area?

....

CS-2. What is the name of the lobby fountain?

....

CS-3. After whom is the gift shop named?

....

CS-4. At what time does the Iguana Arcade close?

....

CS-5. How many steps does the Pyramid of the Sun at the Dig Site have?

....

CS-6. What are the three guest room areas of the resort?

....

CS-7. What is the name of the cantina at the main pool?

....

CS-8. What unusual item can you crawl through at the Dig Site?

....

CS-9. What is the name of the large lake in the center of the resort?

....

CS-10. How many pool areas are at the resort?

....

CS-11. What is the statue of Jose Carioca holding in Panchito's?

....

CS-12. What sort of beast inhabits the dome in the lobby?

....

CS-13. Where can you find a large lizard climbing a wall?

....

Resorts
Coronado Springs
✠ ✠ & ✠ ✠ ✠

CS-14. What is the Lost City of Cibola?

CS-15. What are the two main items available for rent at "La Marina"?

CS-16. What color is the astroturf lining the edge of the volleyball court?

CS-17. How many guests can a large "Water Bee" accomodate?

CS-18. What is the name of the road that circles the resort?

CS-19. What fountain is located between the Pepper Market and Francisco's?

CS-20. Name the brand of citrus fruit that's advertised above the seating in the Pepper Market.

CS-21. What is the person in the Siesta's sign doing?

CS-22. What is spitting water at the fountain near Casita #3?

CS-23. The slide at the Dig Site is named for what cat?

CS-24. What is the first rule at the Lost City of Cibola?

CS-25. What item is at the bottom of the Coronado Springs emblem?

CS-26. Where can you see a "bean" playing maracas?

Resorts
Fort Wilderness

FW-1. What colors are the three internal bus routes?

....

FW-2. What company displays an RV (recreational vehicle) at the Settlement Trading Post?

....

FW-3. After whom is the Settlement Arcade named?

....

FW-4. After whom is the Meadow Arcade named?

....

FW-5. What is the name of camping loop 2500?

....

FW-6. What camping loop is Wagon Wheel Way?

....

FW-7. What is Donald wearing on his head at the Meadow Trading Post?

....

FW-8.

AllEars® Mousy Mindboggler

The food we serve's not fancy chow
But folks who come here sure say "Wow!"
They like our grub, our prices better
Eat your fill—don't become a debtor.

We're surely off the beaten trail
To get here you need to ride or sail
You could probably even ride a horse
You'd have to get it here first, of course.

Once you're here there's more to do
Than try our grub—there are fun things, too
So venture over to try our eats
And sample the nearby non-food treats.

What is this and where is it located?

....

Resorts
Fort Wilderness
✠ ✠ & ✠ ✠ ✠

FW-9. Where do you group camp at Fort Wilderness?

....

FW-10. What type of pills does Herrick's make?

....

FW-11. What is the name of the corral at the
Tri Circle-D Ranch?

....

FW-12. How many water slides are at the Meadow
swimming pool?

....

FW-13. A tree named after what yard tool can be found
between Crockett's Tavern and the Marina?

....

FW-14. What feed company's sign is prominently
displayed at the Settlement Trading Post?

....

FW-15. A court for what sport is at the entrance to
Little Bear Path?

....

FW-16. What is the name of the trail directly across
from the Meadow Trading Post?

....

FW-17. How much is the reward for Sam Bass?

....

FW-18. Between the Campfire Show and Meadow
swimming pool are courts for what game?

....

FW-19. What "World Renowned" doctor advertises at
the campfire show ring?

....

FW-20. How long has Clover King Supply Company
been pushing West?

....

Resorts
Grand Floridian

✠

GF-1. What is atop the turrets of the resort buildings?

....

GF-2. What shape is the Summerhouse?

....

GF-3. What is the phone extension at the bus stop?

....

GF-4. What is the name of the tennis courts?

....

GF-5. The path to the tennis courts passes through which monorail pylon?

....

GF-6. What boat flag color launches from the marina?

....

GF-7. What is at the top of the 1900 Park Fare sign?

....

GF-8. From what year is the squirrel cage?

....

GF-9. How many stained glass domes are in the ceiling of the Grand Lobby?

....

GF-10.

AllEars® Mousy Mindboggler

I'm long and sleek
Some would say I'm streamlined
I have twelve different colors
Among them is lime.

Even though I am speedy
I don't ever fly
Yet the best way to see me
Is to look toward the sky.

Who or what am I?

....

Resorts
Grand Floridian
✠ ✠ & ✠ ✠ ✠

GF-11. Who manufactures the clock and thermometer at the theme pool?

GF-12. What is the monorail beam clearance at the Grand Floridian Spa?

GF-13. What extension would you call to reserve the Grand 1?

GF-14. At the pool behind the main building (the one without the water slide), what is the depth of the water to the left of the lifeguard chair?

GF-15. What is the Grand 1's home port?

GF-16. On the second floor, there is a painting titled "Florida Citrus Fruit 1910." What is on Tab 22?

GF-17. What year is the metal Ferris Wheel from?

GF-18. What is the name of the studio in front of the Wedding Pavilion?

GF-19. What shopping is available on the Windsor Level?

GF-20. What year was the "Statistical Map of Florida" published?

GF-21. From what year is the American Barber Pole?

GF-22. In Mizner's Lounge, what subject does Volume 5 of "Beacon Lights of History" cover?

GF-23. Where is Katie's Cove?

Resorts
Old Key West

✠

OK-1. How many parrots are in the mural behind the check-in desk?

....

OK-2. What color is the eel on The Electric Eel?

....

OK-3. What's the name of the exercise room?

....

OK-4. What colors are the lighthouse near the Hospitality House?

....

OK-5. What does the pool slide at the theme pool resemble?

....

OK-6. What is the common bond of the people in the photos that cover the walls near Olivia's Restaurant?

....

OK-7. What is above the mountains in the logo on the Old Key West entrance sign?

....

OK-8. What is the Gurgling Suitcase?

....

OK-9. Where in Old Key West can you find the image photographed below?

....

Old Key West
✠ ✠ & ✠ ✠ ✠

OK-10. What's the name of the reading room?

OK-11. Which governor has a sign at the Olivia's Restaurant podium?

OK-12. What's written in Latin around the Community Hall emblem?

OK-13. Where can you get shuffleboard equipment?

OK-14. What is the maximum capacity of a ferry boat?

OK-15. From what year is the blue nose model found in Conch Flats General Store?

OK-16. What's the machine location information for the arcade?

OK-17. Who makes the clear green turtle soup advertised on the K.W. Electric Company Car?

OK-18. Where is Turtle Krawl according to the phone guide found there?

OK-19. Who manufactered typewriter #7?

Captain's Corner

I spent the greater part of the summer at the old Isle of Bones, as it is known by some. It is an easy sail from my Fish Cafe at the Marketplace. During an exploration one, day I discovered Grandy's soup in the Hospitality House. You might think it was at Olivia's, but in fact it is closer to Pappa's.

Resorts
Polynesian

✠

PL-1. How many drums are in the garden at the main entrance?

....

PL-2. What year did the Polynesian open?

....

PL-3. What's the name of the store across from Captain Cook's?

....

PL-4. What number do you dial from a house phone for the marina?

....

PL-5. What art gallery is located in the Great Ceremonial House?

....

PL-6. Which fairy can be found in the glass etching outside Captain Cook's?

....

PL-7. What color are the feet on the Barefoot Bar's menu?

....

PL-8. What is the name of the Boat Rental shop at the marina?

....

PL-9.

AllEars® Mousy Mindboggler

In this lush and tropic place
You might feel a gentle breeze
As you sip from your pineapple
You look out on lots of trees.

Do you hear the parrots singing?
They're calling merrily
Come up and join us for a bite
Where we're all Family.

What am I?

....

Resorts
Polynesian
✠ ✠ & ✠ ✠ ✠

PL-10. What's located inside the pool volcano?

PL-11. What is the sixth rule of the quiet pool?

PL-12. What kind of spoonbill is pictured across from the phones by the first floor ladies' restroom in the Great Ceremonial House?

PL-13. According to the sign, how high is the roof over the covered loading/unloading area outside the Great Ceremonial House?

PL-14. What three buildings do you pass per the map, when you travel from the second floor of the Great Ceremonial House to the Luau Cove?

PL-15. What are the hours of the Concierge Lounge?

PL-16. What three famous nephews are wearing grass skirts in Trader Jack's?

PL-17. What inspection area can be found by the coolers in Samoa Snacks?

PL-18. What character is on the Kona Kid's menu displayed outside Kona Cafe?

PL-19. Kona Cafe advertises "To taste the perfect cup" and also to stir what?

PL-20. What is a Funky Monkey served in?

PL-21. What was King David La'ameakalakua' also know as?

PL-22. When will the customs officials return from lunch?

Pop Century

✠

PC-1. A statue of Lady from "Lady and the Tramp" can be found at the Bowling Pin pool. What shape is the charm on her collar?

....

PC-2. What song is "H1" on the Bowling Pin pool jukebox?

....

PC-3. Roger Rabbit is standing on something in front of the keyboard to the Computer pool. What is it?

....

PC-4. How many function keys are on the keyboard at the Computer pool?

....

PC-5. What color elephant is sticking out of the Play-Doh can at the Hippy Dippy pool?

....

PC-6. Who makes Imperial Yo-Yo's?

....

PC-7. What film won the Academy Award for Best Picture in 1977?

....

PC-8. Where is the Hidden Mickey in Everything Pop!?

This one floored me! — Jack

....

PC-9. What are the three Walt Disney World icons you can see on the horizon while walking about this resort?

....

PC-10. What color are the size 11 bowling shoes at the Bowling Pin pool?

....

PC-11. What color purse does Mrs. Potato Head carry?

....

Resorts

Pop Century
✠ ✠ & ✠ ✠ ✠

PC-12. What year did the Sears Tower open?

PC-13. What two Disney characters overlook the Hippy Dippy pool?

PC-14. In what year did Mount Saint Helens erupt?

PC-15. What Utah license plate is found in the shadowbox case in the check-in lobby?

PC-16. What two movies are playing in the drive-in photo behind the check-in desk?

PC-17. In the photo murals behind the check-in desk, in what decade does the first color photograph appear?

PC-18. What Disneyland attraction has a board game in one of the lobby displays?

PC-19. Whose slogan was "The Power is Within Your Reach"?

PC-20. Who wrote "Girl in the Curl: A Century of Women in Surfing"?

PC-21. In what year was the Salk vaccine invented?

PC-22. What CD soundtrack appears in a shadowbox display?

PC-23. Who created the Gateway Memorial Arch?

PC-24. Who invented the Koosh Ball?

PC-25. Who wrote Plaid Passion?

Resorts
Port Orleans

We've combined the two sister resorts that make up Port Orleans—French Quarter and Riverside. In the easy questions below, the first five answers are found in French Quarter, followed by the next five answers in Riverside.

PO-1. What's on the corner of Rue D' Baga and Neptune's Parade at French Quarter?

PO-2. What's the name of the larger slide at the French Quarter playground?

PO-3. In the French Quarter courtyard between Rue D' Baga and Grand D' Toure, there is a reflecting pool. How many spitting frogs are there?

PO-4. What does the mural behind the check-in counter at French Quarter show?

PO-5. Where can you find giant ice cream cones, a huge crown, and whopper-sized beads at French Quarter?

PO-6. Boatwright's Dining Hall's main sign at Riverside is on what?

PO-7. In front of which Riverside building is a pretty white gazebo?

PO-8. In the Riverside Mill, you'll find a statue of a Native American. In what shape is the black pattern on the top of his moccasins?

PO-9. What can you get at the River Roost at Riverside, according to its sign?

PO-10. Where is the butterfly garden at Riverside?

Resorts
Port Orleans
✠ ✠ & ✠ ✠ ✠

PO-11. What's the location (physical, not mailing) of the arcade?

....

PO-12. What year was the Riverside Mill established?

....

PO-13. What's the bathing load of the wading pool at Port Orleans Riverside?

....

PO-14. What's the maximum occupancy of Sassagoula Floatworks?

....

PO-15. The bridge to Ol' Man Island (from Riverside Mill and Market) was established when?

....

PO-16. What's the maximum recommended time for the hot tub at the French Quarter pool?

....

PO-17. Who settled Ol' Man Island?

....

PO-18. Royal Baking Power is _____, _____, _____.

....

PO-19. What is the logo of French Quarter building #5?

....

PO-20. What times do the Steamships arrive from Memphis?

....

PO-21. What's the address of French Quarter building #4?

....

PO-22. At the French Quarter, what building's symbol is a trombone?

....

Resorts

Saratoga Springs

✠

SS-1. How many horse pictures are in the kid's TV lounge in the check-in area at the Carriage House?

....

SS-2. What is remarkable about the horse in the middle of the check-in area?

....

SS-3. What Disney character is standing in the middle of the pop jet play fountain?

....

SS-4. How many Mickeys are on the pink jockey silks (jacket)?

....

SS-5. What's interesting about the framed rack of pool balls in The Turf Club?

....

SS-6. What golf course is at Saratoga Springs?

....

SS-7. What are the hours of the spa by the main pool?

....

SS-8. What is the name of the main pool?

....

SS-9. Where can you find the spitting frog pictured below?

....

Resorts

Saratoga Springs
✠ ✠ & ✠ ✠ ✠

SS-10. What is "On the Rocks"?

....

SS-11. What can you rent at Horsing Around?

....

SS-12. The Paddock is along what street?

....

SS-13. To what frequency do you set your radio to hear the far left TV in the fitness room?

....

SS-14. How many fish are on the fountain outside the arcade area guest laundry?

....

SS-15. Who was Prince Phillip's horse in Sleeping Beauty?

....

SS-16. What kind of peppermint animal can you purchase at Saratoga Springs?

....

SS-17. What is the color number of the blue used in the Saratoga Springs Donald Duck's outfit?

....

SS-18. In Reminiscences of Saratoga Lake, how many racing boats are on the water?

....

SS-19. What running of the Travers took place in Saratoga in 2002?

....

SS-20. What hotel can you find in the registration area? (Hint: It isn't Saratoga Springs!)

....

SS-21. How many horses are in the Saratoga Springs Carousel picture?

....

Resorts
Swan and Dolphin

✠

SD-1. What color are the flags that top the walkway between the Swan and Dolphin?

....

SD-2. Are there televisions at the Swan bus stop?

....

SD-3. At the fountains throughout the first floor of the Swan, how many swans are at each fountain?

....

SD-4. On what floor is the Royal Beach Club Lounge?

....

SD-5. What bird has ten rooms at the Swan Convention Center?

....

SD-6. How many dolphin fish are on top of the Dolphin?

....

SD-7. What color tile makes the W/M pattern at the main entrance to the Dolphin?

....

SD-8. What is in Daisy's Garden at the Dolphin?

....

SD-9. What animal is in the sandbox at the playground?

....

SD-10.

AllEars® Mousy Mindboggler

I'm someplace new in someplace older
I once was plain but now I'm bolder.

I specialize in fruits of the sea
But you can have anything when you visit me.

You might think my owner is proper and prim
But that's just his name, no reflection on him.

What am I and where do you find me?

....

Resorts
Swan and Dolphin
✠ ✠ & ✠ ✠ ✠

SD-11. What are the hours of the Shipping Desk at the Swan?

SD-12. Out by the east elevators there are three desks: conceirge, ticketing, and what else?

SD-13. What's the occupancy of the Swan Game Room?

SD-14. According to the Dining and Entertainment Guide in the Lobby, does the Garden Grove Cafe accept reservations?

SD-15. What is the name of the pool with the slide and waterfall?

SD-16. What kind of boats have a dock by the beach volleyball nets?

SD-17. What Magic Kingdom attraction comes to mind when you look up at the Swan lobby ceiling?

SD-18. Where can you find a jukebox at the Dolphin?

SD-19. What's in a "Pool Level"? (Hint: It's not water.)

SD-20. A sign for Carro Amano Aranci Gold Buckle Association from East Highlands, California, is located where?

SD-21. What's the e-mail address for the WDW Swan & Dolphin Hotel Executive's Business Centers?

SD-22. What is the operating address of the Dolphin?

Resorts
Wilderness Lodge

✠

WL-1. Who is at the bottom of the Eagle Pole, according to the plaque?

....

WL-2. If you want to take a bus to Fort Wilderness, which bus stop do you want?

....

WL-3. How many bells are outside the Buttons and Bells Game Arcade?

....

WL-4. Who makes the mailbox outside the Mercantile?

....

WL-5. What Disney character is on top of the totem pole outside the Mercantile?

....

WL-6. What toys are available to play with in the Whispering Canyon Cafe waiting area?

....

WL-7. What is on the center table of the Villas rotunda?

....

WL-8. What animal is on the elevator doors to the fifth floor of the Villas?

....

WL-9.

AllEars® Mousy Mindboggler

I'm not on a ride, not in a show
I'm in the wilderness, don't you know?

I have a counterpart way out West
But the faithful here know that I'm the best

You can set your watch by me, it's true
Just keep your distance until I'm through!

What's my name and where do you find me?

....

Resorts
Wilderness Lodge
✠ ✠ & ✠ ✠ ✠

WL-10. What's the name of the falls leading into the main pool?

WL-11. From what century is the crow headdress (the one facing Fire Rock) in the lobby?

WL-12. Where will you find the Unitah and Henry mountain ranges on a map at the resort?

WL-13. Who's prospecting in Nevada on the Scenic Line of the West map in the Villas?

WL-14. Who's got the best sleeping this side of the Mississippi?

WL-15. What's the extension of the house phone in the Iron Spike Room?

WL-16. Who built the Carrolwood Pacific Cars?

WL-17. What fossils from the Grand Canyon are on the fourth floor fireplace display?

WL-18. Walt was named an honorary engineer of what engine?

WL-19. What is the raven on top of the Raven Pole doing, according to the plaque?

WL-20. Where will you find the Lost Lake shown in this photograph?

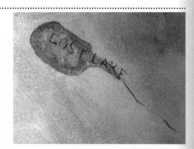

Resorts
Yacht & Beach Club

✠

YB-1. Who is piloting the boat at the main entrance at Fittings and Fairings?

YB-2. From what year is the globe in the Yacht Club lobby?

YB-3. According to the sign, how long is the dry time at the guest laundry located at the Yacht Club guest pool?

YB-4. Besides wheels and anchors, what other symbol can be found in the Yacht Club guest laundry room curtains?

YB-5. What number do you call for an appointment at Periwig Salon?

YB-6. What are the ages of children who may participate in the Sandcastle Club?

YB-7. How many candles are in each sconce at the Beach Club lobby?

YB-8. Where can you buy gelato?

YB-9.

AllEars® Mousy Mindboggler

We are not just the sands of time
We never shift our shape
We're definitely at Disney World
And yet we're near the Cape.
If you look close, you'll likely spot
The Mouse within our reach
We can be found upon dry land
And yet we're at the Beach.

What are we and where can you find us?

Resorts
Yacht & Beach Club
✠ ✠ & ✠ ✠ ✠

YB-10. What are the three gauges on the Mahogany ship's helm station, circa 1920?

....

YB-11. What's the name of the slide in the Albatross?

....

YB-12. What's the depth of the water between the two waterfalls outside of Ship Shape?

....

YB-13. What sign, other than the Crew's Cup Lounge's own sign, can you find at the entrance to the Crew's Cup Lounge?

....

YB-14. In the main hall of the convention center, there is a large painting. How many boats are visible?

....

YB-15. What flower is depicted in the stained glass picture in the window by Ariel near the entrance to the Drawing Room?

....

YB-16. How many Atlantic hot air balloons are depicted in the mural behind the Disney Cruise Line desk?

....

YB-17. Who is the builder of the American Clipper Ship Nightengale?

....

YB-18. Who was the division coordinator for Walt Disney World Company's United Way campaign in 1994?

....

YB-19. What number is on the blue CFC flag?

....

YB-20. What is in a "Stormalong"? (Hint: It is not water.)

....

YB-21. According to the wine map of California, what section is Glen Ellen in?

....

Disney Cruise Line's
Disney Magic
✠

"If I were still upon the seas, a treasure hunter I would be. I'd dig up silver and dig up gold, and oh what Magic there is to behold!"—Captain Skatt's skit at the talent show

DM-1. How many buttons are on the hand holding up the Mickey Slide?

....

DM-2. Stateroom 8030 is also known as what?

....

DM-3. What three clubs are found on Beat Street?

....

DM-4. The ice cream spot on deck 9 is known as what?

....

DM-5. The door immediately to the right of stateroom 6000 has what sign on it?

....

DM-6. A map of what island is on the forward staircase between decks 4 and 5?

....

DM-7. What color is the "Y" in the signs for Mickey's Mates?

....

DM-8. The restroom sign on Beat Street is made to look like what kind of traffic device?

....

DM-9. Who is featured on the statue outside Lumiere's?

....

DM-10. What game is mounted in the first shadowbox on the left when you enter Diversions?

....

DM-11. What is the name of the arcade?

....

DM-12. Where can you find the image pictured in the photo to the right?

....

Disney Cruise Line's
Disney Magic

✠

DM-13. According to the manhole covers, in what year was Beat Street established?

....

DM-14. What color are Goofy's gloves in the mural at the Mickey Pool?

....

DM-15. What logo is at the center of Beat Street's manhole covers?

....

DM-16. What hangs from the center chandeliers in Parrot Cay?

....

DM-17. On the aft staircase between decks 3 and 4, what is the top card in the Magician Mickey photo?

....

DM-18. What pizzeria is on deck 9?

....

DM-19. What hangs from the center chandeliers in Lumiere's?

....

DM-20. What letter is the last row of the Buena Vista Theatre?

....

DM-21. Who is riding a jet ski on the bow of the Magic?

....

DM-22. Where can you find the image pictured in the photo below?

....

Disney Cruise Line's
Disney Magic
✠ ✠

DM-23. What is the significance of the red and blue arrows in the carpet of the stateroom passageways?

DM-24. Where will you find a sketch from the film "Musicland"?

DM-25. On deck 6 midship, there is a large mural. What paper is the gentleman reading?

DM-26. On the midship stairway on deck 3 is a picture of various sea creatures. What type of coral is shown?

DM-27. What firelocker is located on deck 1 midship, between the two staircases?

DM-28. What stateroom is the Roy O. Disney Suite?

DM-29. The deck 8 midship elevator lobby has a limited edition print. Out of the 125 prints made, what number is this one?

DM-30. On the midship stairway on deck 3 is a map of constellations. Who are the triplets?

DM-31. Scenes from what "How To" film can be found in the forward staircase between decks 6 and 7?

DM-32. How many tables have inlaid chess/checkerboards in Diversions?

DM-33. What is in the center of the Topsider Buffet sign?

DM-34. The Internet Cafe is located beside what lounge?

Disney Cruise Line's
Disney Magic
✠ ✠ ✠

DM-35. How many life preservers are on the aft overlook on deck 7?

DM-36. On deck 5 between the atrium and the Buena Vista Theatre, there are pictures of characters from what feature film?

DM-37. What bridge can be found between decks 4 and 5 on the aft staircase?

DM-38. Who reports the latest cruise news? (Hint: It's a Disney character.)

DM-39. In what year was the cartoon "Boat Builders" made?

DM-40. In the mural found on deck 6 midship, Mickey and Minnie are shown. What character's clothes are also shown, but without the character?

DM-41. In what year was the cartoon "Bellboy Donald" made?

DM-42. When did the Blues Brothers play at the Chateau Inn in Buffalo, NY?

DM-43. If you stand all the way forward on deck 10 and look straight up, what do you see?

DM-44. What character is featured in the story sketches for "Baggage Buster"?

DM-45. Where will you find portholes into the galley (kitchen)?

Disney Cruise Line's
Disney Wonder

✠

DW-1. What pair of animals are woven into the carpet on deck 9 forward, near the elephants?

....

DW-2. What is the depth of the Goofy Pool?

....

DW-3. What is in Pluto's dog bowl?

....

DW-4. Which Disney character has a bronze statue in the atrium?

....

DW-5. What five beach items are on the Beach Blanket Buffet sign?

....

DW-6. What shape is the message holder above each stateroom's number plaque?

....

DW-7. What pattern is on the carpet inside Beach Blanket Buffet?

....

DW-8. On deck 9, there is a mural of Goofy floating in an inner tube. What is he wearing that seems out of place?

....

DW-9. What color is Pinocchio's bowtie?

....

DW-10. Where is the image pictured below found?

....

Disney Cruise Line's
Disney Wonder
✠ ✠

DW-11. What is the yellow fish beside King Triton doing in Triton's restaurant?

DW-12. What is the atrium chandelier primarily made of?

DW-13. What forms the word "Club" in the Oceaneer Club?

DW-14. What images are carved in the back of the chairs at Parrot Cay?

DW-15. What is the black musical instrument depicted on the aft wall of the Internet Cafe?

DW-16. What are Huey, Duey, and Louie wearing in Mickey's Mates?

DW-17. Where is the Medical Health Center?

DW-18. Who adorns the bow of the ship?

DW-19. What is the tall, gold statue inside Studio Sea?

DW-20. Where is the image pictured below found?

Disney Cruise Line's
Disney Wonder
✠ ✠

DW-21. What is the "QuarterMaster" holding?

DW-22. Where was the Disney Wonder constructed?

DW-23. Where will you still find gas for 32 cents a gallon?

DW-24. What is pictured on the Studio Sea door, midship entrance?

DW-25. How many pools are on the Disney Wonder and where are they?

DW-26. What is etched into the window above Treasure Ketch?

DW-27. How many public women's restrooms are on deck 4 alone?

DW-28. What is the only deck that passengers cannot walk the length of from forward to aft?

DW-29. What number appears on the giant paintbrushes in Animator's Palate?

DW-30. What is the shape of the porthole above Mickey's Mates shop?

DW-31. Where can you find carpet with this pattern?

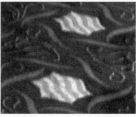

Disney Cruise Line's
Disney Wonder
✠ ✠ ✠

DW-32. A "secret passage" exists on deck 5. What is it and who is it for?

DW-33. Where will you find Goofy eating a hot dog?

DW-34. Where are photos of both versions of the "Fab Four" walking across Abbey Road?

DW-35. On what side of the ship will you find "Walnut Canyon:" port or starboard?

DW-36. Where on the ship will you find an area called "Ovations"?

DW-37. Where is Assembly Station T?

DW-38. Where will you find a picture of a yellow-jacketed jockey riding a black horse?

DW-39. Which Mickey ear is intended for children wearing swim diapers: port or starboard?

DW-40. A mild, gentle breeze from the west is know as what?

DW-41. Which of the Disney stage shows includes Quasimodo, the Hunchback of Notre Dame?

DW-42. Which Disney character is holding a rope in the shape of Mickey's head?

DW-43. Where will you find a billboard with Walt Disney on it?

Disney Cruise Line's
Castaway Cay

✠

CC-1. What is in the bottles in front of the post office?

....

CC-2. What is the big fish using as bait to get his "Fresh Catch"?

....

CC-3. What are the four characters on the Mount Rustmore buoys?

....

CC-4. How many minutes does it take to walk from the Scuttle Cove tram stop to the Palm Central Station tram stop?

....

CC-5. On the First Aid navigational sign near Scuttle Cove, what is on the finger of the pointing hand?

....

CC-6. What Disney character appears on the Relay Bay sign?

....

CC-7. What color is the fish on Gil's Fins • Boats near the snorkel lagoon?

....

CC-8. What symbol indicates artifacts on the snorkel trail map?

....

CC-9. What kind of plates are nailed to the rafters of the Conched Out bar?

....

CC-10. Who is the captain of the shrimp distributors?

....

CC-11. What does "Suns" and "Daughters" mean on Castaway Cay?

....

CC-12. Where can you play pool on Castaway Cay?

....

CC-13. What is Donald holding on the side of the abandoned plane on the air strip?

....

Disney Cruise Line's
Castaway Cay
✠ ✠ & ✠ ✠ ✠

CC-14. What three things did the three Castaway Cay explorers find?

....

CC-15. What is the elevation at Mount Rustmore?

....

CC-16. What is the street address of the Stauffer Trawling Co.?

....

CC-17. Who is May B. Tamara?

....

CC-18. Who is the proprietor of Chandlery & General Stores?

....

CC-19. What kind of collection belongs to Mike & Mike?

....

CC-20. What number appears in the upper left corner of Johnson's West Indies map?

....

CC-21. What are the tents at Scuttles' Cove called?

....

CC-22. Where is Skylar's Hunky Dory?

....

CC-23. What do you get free with 10,000 gallons of gas?

....

CC-24. What is the weight of the "fresh catch"?

....

CC-25. Complete this sentence: "Please be aware of ocean conditions which may involve but are not limited to..."

....

CC-26. What was the occupation of the explorer who discovered a "timeless recipe for good health"?

....

Walt Disney World's
Typhoon Lagoon

✠

"A curious hunt once roared cross the bay, catching folks in its grasp, eager to play. Instead of hanging out in their resort room, this book swept them to Typhoon Lagoon."—Silly poem by Captain Skatt, inspired by a visit to Typhoon Lagoon

TL-1. What boat is stranded on top of Mt. Mayday behind Typhoon Lagoon?

TL-2. What is the current wave condition at Typhoon Lagoon?

TL-3. What is Placid Palms now known as?

TL-4. Whose mailbox is outside of the Board Room?

TL-5. How many slides comprise the Humunga Cowabunga attraction?

TL-6. What is the scientific name of "Really Big Shark"?

TL-7. What color are the lights in the shipwreck viewing area of the Shark Reef attraction?

TL-8. What number do you call to learn to surf at Craig Carroll's Surf School?

TL-9. How deep is Castaway Creek?

TL-10. How often does the boat on Mt. Mayday shoot off water?

Captain's Corner

A thorough exploration of this storm-torn area revealed an odd little shack on the beach. It called itself a "board" room. The shack held many interesting items and is well worth another visit.

Walt Disney World's
Typhoon Lagoon
✠ ✠ & ✠ ✠ ✠

TL-11. Where is Tropical Amity Fruit Exporters?

....

TL-12. Complete this sentence: "Instead of a _____
___ _____ _____, the wind swept them here to
Typhoon Lagoon."

....

TL-13. What surfing magazine is found on the "desk" of
the Board Room?

....

TL-14. What does the "boat 4 sale" at the Typhoon
Boatworks need?

....

TL-15. What's the number for the marooned boat by
Singaport Sal's?

....

TL-16. What is the depth of the Keelhaul Falls catch
pool?

....

TL-17. What marine supply company supplies the
Typhoon Lagoon Boatworks?

....

TL-18. What won't get washed at the Ketchakiddie
Creek boat wash?

....

TL-19. What is Ms. Tilly's home port?

....

TL-20. Who played Freddie in Bikini Beach Blanket
Muscle Party Bingo?

....

TL-21. What is the Pineapple Plunger?

....

TL-22. What song by the Beach Gators is everyone's
favorite at the Board Room?

....

TL-23. Where was "the big one that got away" found?

....

Walt Disney World's
Blizzard Beach

✠

"Nothing's finer than being stuck in a blizzard with a treasure hunt and a big lizard."—Captain Skatt's T-shirt

BB-1. What are the two pink flamingos doing on the roof?

BB-2. What is the alligator in the Blizzard Beach logo wearing?

BB-3. There's a snowfamily in Blizzard Beach, complete with a snowdaddy and snowmommy. What is the cute snowboy's name?

BB-4. What is the tallest slide in Blizzard Beach?

BB-5. How many flags are at the very top of the ski jump?

BB-6. Where is the snowcastle fountain?

BB-7. How many lanes are there on the Toboggan Racer slide?

BB-8.

AllEars® Mousy Mindboggler

Ubiquitous is what I am
I'm nearly everywhere, in every park on every street
You want me and I'm there!

Some say that I am made of stone
It only seems that way, until I'm set free in your hand
And that's after you pay.

I'm shaped just like our favorite mouse
But I don't linger long, my ears are first to disappear
Soon after that I'm gone!

What am I?

Walt Disney World's
Blizzard Beach
✠ ✠ & ✠ ✠ ✠

BB-9. What slide at Blizzard Beach times each rider's descent so you can compete with your friends?

....

BB-10. What is the name of the mountain at Blizzard Beach?

....

BB-11. Typhoon Lagoon has the Laguna Gator mascot. What is the name of Blizzard Beach's mascot?

....

BB-12. How many of the Runoff Rapids slides are limited to single riders?

....

BB-13. How tall is Summit Plummet?

....

BB-14. Complete this sentence: Sonny's Sled says "Buy Now, _____ Later."

....

BB-15. What is the elevation of Blizzard Beach's mountain?

....

BB-16. What shape is carved out of the green shutters on the chalet just under the ski jump?

....

BB-17. What is mounted under each chair lift?

....

BB-18. Where does the park's mascot live?

....

BB-19. Where will you find a fireplace with a familiar three-circle shape above it?

....

BB-20. Complete this sentence: "When you think snow, think ____ _____."

....

BB-21. Where will you find a "hidden alligator" sunning itself?

....

Make Your Own Treasure Hunt

We have a little confession—we think it's as much fun to create treasure hunts as it is to play them. Why do you think we wrote this book? Not only do you notice more details when you're creating a hunt, but you can tailor it to your needs—easier for kids, more devious for a challenger. As a "huntmaster," you can even create special themed hunts for important occasions like a birthday, marriage proposal, or holiday. Or maybe you need a break from all those rides and want to do something new and different. Whatever your reasons, there's a treasure hunt for it.

Getting the Questions

It's hard to create a hunt if you don't know what to put in it. No one has everything in the parks committed to memory, and most folks want to find new things rather than well-known trivia that can be answered from memory. If you have the opportunity to visit the parks to create your treasure hunt, you can create a question for just about everything you'll find. We do recommend you stick to questions that have a clear, definite answer that isn't likely to change by the time you play your treasure hunt. Thus, you'll want to avoid holiday-related items, entertainers, items that are not likely to be unique, and things that are likely to change, like park hours and restaurant menus. We also strongly recommend you avoid the temptation to hide items or clues at the parks. Your items may "walk off" before you can actually play, or they may simply get swept up by Disney's cast members.

Finding Questions on the Fly

If you can't visit the parks before the treasure hunt, try an "On-The-Fly Hunt" with two or more people. Just go to a park and split up. Give each person (or team) the task of finding a set of questions in different places. For example, one team could find three questions in each World Showcase East pavilion, while the other team goes for the West side. You then meet in the middle at a prearranged time and place and swap questions. Each team hunts for the answers to the questions dug up by the other team. This allows for fun in both collecting and answering the questions!

Make Your Own Hunts (continued)

If you can dream it, you can probably find it!

If you have neither the time to visit a park before your hunt nor to make up a hunt on the fly, there's still hope! Try making of list of items you would expect to see at Disney and see how many you can find when you arrive. For example, if you are visiting during the holidays, create a list of interesting holiday-related items to find, such as a gingerbread house and a menorah. Your item list can be as simple or complicated as you wish. If you want a more challenging hunt, create a list of unusual items, such as a New York license plate (found somewhere in a park, not a parking lot), a bullwhip, and a steamer trunk with a Hilton Head sticker on it.

Have camera, will hunt!

If you have digital cameras (or camcorders), try a hunt for specific places in a park or a hotel. Jennifer and husband Dave created a photo hunt where teams had to go around the Seven Seas Lagoon (Magic Kingdom, Contemporary, Polynesian, and Grand Floridian), finding locations and snapping group shots at each one. If you know the park well, you could make a list of places without too much effort. Otherwise, just combine this hunt with the ideas in the above paragraph, and have folks hunt for photos with things they're likely to find. For example, you can get a photo taken with a cast member, at a water fountain, on a train, or by a statue. You can add in a bit of fun by requiring that the participants pose a certain way in each picture. This hunt makes for great photo souvenirs, too!

Traditional group hunts

Here's how Jennifer and Dave go about making a hunt for a group of people. First, they plan when and where it will be, so good questions can be scouted beforehand. For example, they would collect questions in September for a treasure hunt in December during MouseFest. It works best to set aside an afternoon to scour the chosen location for likely questions and answers. Then Jennifer and Dave split up and write down everything they can think of and even take pictures of some items they may find hard to recall later. When they return from their trip, they look at all the notes and compile a list of questions from the best ideas. The questions are printed out to distribute right before the start of the hunt—the answers are listed on another sheet for easy scoring. It also helps to have rules for the hunt (feel free to borrow those listed in this book), a theme for the hunt, and an appropriate prize or two.

What Makes a Good Hunt?

We believe a good hunt presents a challenge without being frustrating, leaves time for fun and companionship, and shows the participants things they may never have noticed before. Everyone has to enjoy themselves, even if there can only be one "winner." Seriously consider whether you want your hunters to stand in queues or ride an attraction, as that can take a lot of time or force them on a ride they'd rather not experience. Always consider how the hunt may affect other guests and Disney cast members—no one should cause a disturbance while hunting. Time and walking distances are also a factor. For all but the most exhausting hunts, we suggest you limit your hunt to one or two small areas of a park, rather than the entire park. Not only is it easier on the hunters, but it's much easier for the "huntmaster" to oversee the fun.

Consider the complexity of your hunt. It's difficult to judge in advance how easy or difficult to make your hunt. Take a good look at your audience and determine what they'd be most comfortable with—an easy, fun diversion or a sadistic, difficult challenge. Most beginners prefer to just have a good time and may not want to be too competitive.

If your hunt involves definite answers, make sure you know all the answers and—more specifically—exactly where and how a hunter would find them. At the end of your hunt, you'll want to be able to differentiate the good answers from the bad. You may also need to explain the location of a few of your answers to hunters who were unsuccessful at locating them. We suggest you keep very good notes on all answer locations—you may even want to take photographs of each one!

Rewards and Prizes

For many, the challenge of the hunt is the reward. Others may need a bit more motivation. Pick rewards and prizes in line with your hunt and/or group. For a traditional prize, you may find Mickey "trophies" on Hollywood Boulevard at Disney-MGM Studios (they look a bit like Oscar statues) or on the Disney cruise ships (they are called "Golden Mickeys" here). Gift certificates and meals are easy, no-fuss prizes. Or why not let your winner choose the date of your next Disney trip?

My Treasure Hunt

Use this space to record your own treasure hunt for a future visit or just for posterity!

MY-1.

....

MY-2.

....

MY-3.

....

MY-4.

....

MY-5.

....

MY-6.

....

MY-7.

....

MY-8.

....

MY-9.

....

MY-10.

....

MY-11.

....

MY-12.

....

PassPorter
Earn-Your-Badge
Treasure Hunt

Love treasure hunting? Ready to show off your searching skills? As an owner of this book, you are eligible to enter this special PassPorter Treasure Hunt and have an opportunity to earn your Official PassPorter Treasure Hunter badge pin (one per book, please). The official rules for the earn-your-badge treasure hunt are below. The hunt questions begin on the next page. Good luck!

Treasure Hunt Rules

1. To enter the PassPorter Earn-Your-Badge Treasure Hunt, you must own a copy of this book so you can remove the entry form on page 155.

2. Complete as much of the treasure hunt as possible before submitting your entry form. You'll want a score of at least 100 points in order to earn your official badge pin.

3. When you are done, make a copy of your answers and send it along with your completed entry form and any other challenge items you've collected to:

> Captain. J. Skatt
> Badge Coordinator
> P.O. Box 3880
> Ann Arbor, MI 48106

Note: We will only accept entries by mail—we cannot process e-mail or phone submissions. (We will accept digital photos by e-mail, but you must also mail in your entry form.)

4. Please allow 4-6 weeks to process your submission. If you score at least 100 points, you'll receive your free official badge pin, and your name will appear on our Treasure Hunter Vault of Fame (http://www.passporter.com/hunts/vault.htm).

5. One free badge pin per copy of this book. Entry forms must be torn from the actual book; copies will not be accepted.

6. Submissions become the property of PassPorter Travel Press and will not be returned.

PassPorter Hunt (continued)

Question Quest

1. Like the folks at PassPorter, Sully loves to guide others to a great adventure. What is Sully's business and where on Main Street is it? (15 points)

....

2. Thanks to Johannes Gutenberg, PassPorter books are printed rather than handwritten! Where in Epcot is a plaque commemorating his invention? (15 points)

....

3. Travel is the name of our game. Where in Disney-MGM Studios is the Venture Travel Service? (15 points)

....

4. PassPorter's parent company, MediaMarx, was incorporated in November 1998. Find something in Asia that shares the same date. (15 points)

....

5. We believe we've spied a PassPorter on this shelf of books (we think it's hidden behind the blue book). Where in Downtown Disney will you find it? (15 points)

....

Scavenge Challenge

Collect these items to send in with your entry form:
- ❏ A photo of you (or your family/group) at one of the answers for questions 1-5 (5 points).
- ❏ An autograph from a princess (1 point), a villain (5 points), Donald Duck (10 points), or Laguna Gator/Ice Gator (20 points).
- ❏ A photo of you next to the map shown on the right (12 points).
- ❏ A postcard mailed from Disney property to your home—stamped, postmarked, and cancelled (15 points). *For an extra 5 points, write a message to Captain Skatt on the postcard.*

Bonus: Pose with a copy of this book in the above photos and you get an extra 5 bonus points per photo!

PassPorter Earn-Your-Badge Treasure Hunt Entry Form

Directions: Complete this entry form with your answers to the questions on the previous page, as well as your personal information and permissions. Tear out the page from the book, put it in an envelope with your challenge items, and mail to Mr. J. Skatt, Badge Coordinator, P.O. Box 3880, Ann Arbor, MI 48106.

Answers to Questions:

1. .... (15 pts)

2. .... (15 pts)

3. .... (15 pts)

4. .... (15 pts)

5. .... (15 pts)

Collected Items (please list items you're including here):
Note: Both print photos and digital photos are acceptable. You can send digital photos on a CD-ROM or e-mail them to captain@passporter.com.

....

....

....

....

Hunter Information:

Name: ....

Address: ....

City, State, Zip: ....

E-mail Address: ....

Phone: ....

❏ Permission granted to list my name and score on the Treasure Hunter Vault of Fame web page.
❏ Permission granted to include any of my submitted photos on the Treasure Hunter Vault of Fame web page or in an upcoming PassPorter publication with proper attribution.
❏ I have read and agree to the Official PassPorter Treasure Hunt rules.

Get Your Hunting License

OK, you got us—you don't actually need a hunting license to go treasure hunting at Disney! This book is all you need. But we would love to have you register with us so we know you have a copy of the book and you're out there discovering the World. Registering also gives you a chance to sign up for our free e-newsletter filled with articles that will improve your hunting skills—there's even a Captain's Corner column with clues and more treasure hunt questions! Your registration is also the perfect place to tell us what you think of the book, including how we can improve it in the future.

You can register your book in less than 60 seconds at:

http://www.passporter.com/register.htm

If you don't have Web access, fill out the registration form below and mail it to: P.O. Box 3880, Ann Arbor, MI 48106.

Name: ....

Address: ....

City, State, Zip: ....

E-mail Address: ....

What do you like most about this book? ....

....

What do you like least about this book? ....

....

What would you like us to add/change/improve in the future?

....

....

Do you have any comments, questions, or suggestions? ....

....

Check for Updates and Changes

Change is inevitable, even expected. Walt Disney World and the Disney Cruise Line are in constant flux. While we have made an effort to choose questions and answers that we feel have "staying power," there will be changes that affect the contents of this book. As we learn about changes that influence the questions and answers in this book, we will post corrections online for you to peruse. We highly recommend you check this update list before you set off on your treasure hunt adventure. You can get the most recent list of changes at http://www.passporter. com/customs/bookupdates.htm.

Reporting Changes

Of course, keeping up with the changes at Walt Disney World is virtually impossible without your help. When you notice something is different from what is printed in this book, please let us know! You can report your news, updates, changes, and corrections at http://www. passporter.com/wdw/report.htm. And if you want to send a supporting photograph or two to accompany your change, please e-mail it to captain@passporter.com.

Have Questions?

We love to hear from you! Alas, due to the thousands of e-mails and hundreds of phone calls we receive each week, we cannot offer personalized help or advice to all our readers. But there's a great way to get your questions answered: Ask your fellow readers! Visit our message boards at http://www.passporterboards.com, join for free, and post your question. In most cases, fellow readers and Disney fans will offer their ideas and experiences! Our message boards also function as an ultimate list of frequently asked questions. Just browsing through to see the answers to other readers' questions will reap untold benefit! This is also a great way to make friends and have fun while planning your vacation. But be careful—our message boards can be addictive!

More PassPorter Guides

PassPorter Walt Disney World Resort

It all started with Walt Disney World (and a mouse)! Our general Walt Disney World guidebook covers everything you need to plan a practically perfect vacation, including fold-out park maps; full-color photos and charts; resort room layout diagrams; KidTips; descriptions, reviews, and ratings for the resorts, parks, attractions, and restaurants; and much more! This edition also includes 14 organizer pockets you can use to plan your trip before you go, hold papers while you're there, and record your memories for when you return. Learn more and order at http://www.passporter.com/wdw, or get a copy at your favorite bookstore. Our Walt Disney World guide is available in a spiral-bound edition (2006 edition ISBN: 1587710277), and a Deluxe Edition in a ring binder with interior pockets is also available (ISBN: 1587710285).

PassPorter's Walt Disney World for Your Special Needs

It's hardly a one-size-fits-all world at Disney's Orlando resort, yet everyone seems to fit. Consider the typical multi-generational family planning a vacation: pregnant and nursing moms, parents with infants, cousins "keeping Kosher," grandparents with declining mobility, a child with food allergies, an uncle struggling with obesity ... everyday people coping with everyday needs. And Walt Disney World does more to accommodate their many needs than just about anyone. You'll see more wheelchairs and electric scooters in Disney parks than you're likely to see anywhere else. If you know to ask, Disney has devices to help a hearing- or vision-impaired guest enjoy a show, park maps and translation devices in six languages, "Special Assistance" passes for children with autism or ADD, a sheltered spot to breastfeed, chefs and waiters schooled to serve a wide spectrum of special dietary needs ... you could fill a book, and indeed, that's what authors Deb Wills and Debra Martin Koma have done! They've prepared more than 400 pages of in-depth information for Walt Disney World vacationers of all abilities, delivering in-depth coverage of every ride, attraction, and resort on Walt Disney World property from a distinctive "special needs" perspective. Learn more at http://www.passporter.com/wdw/specialneeds or get a copy at your favorite bookstore (ISBN: 1587710188).

More PassPorter Guides

PassPorter's Field Guide to the Disney Cruise Line and Its Ports of Call—Fourth Edition
Completely updated for 2006! Get your cruise plans in shipshape with our updated field guide! Authors Jennifer and Dave Marx cover the Disney Cruise Line in incredible detail, including deck plans, stateroom floor plans, original photos, menus, entertainment guides, port/shore excursion details, and plenty of worksheets to help you budget, plan, and record your cruise information. Now in its fourth edition, this is the original and most comprehensive guidebook devoted to the Disney Cruise Line! Learn more and order your copy at http://www.passporter.com/dcl or get a copy at your favorite bookstore (paperback, no PassPockets; ISBN: 1587710307). Also available in a Deluxe Edition with organizer PassPockets (ISBN: 1587710315).

PassPorter Disneyland Resort and Southern California Attractions
New! PassPorter tours the park that started it all. California's Disneyland, Disney's California Adventure, and Downtown Disney get PassPorter's expert treatment, and we throw in Hollywood and Downtown Los Angeles, Universal Studios, San Diego, SeaWorld, the San Diego Zoo and Wild Animal Park, Legoland, and Six Flags Magic Mountain. All this, and PassPorter's famous PassPockets and planning features. Whether you're making the pilgrimage to Disneyland for the big celebration or planning a classic Southern California family vacation, you can't miss. Learn more and order a copy at http://www.passporter.com/dl, or pick it up at your favorite bookstore (ISBN: 1587710048). Also available as a Deluxe Edition in a padded, six-ring binder (ISBN: 1587710056).

To order our books, visit http://www.passporterstore.com or call toll-free 877-929-3273. PassPorter guidebooks are also available in your local bookstore. If you don't see them on the shelf, just ask!

Note: The ISBN codes above apply to our 2005 or 2006 editions. For the latest edition, ask your bookstore to search their database for "PassPorter."

Treasure Chests
(Answers)

You're just itching to see the answers, aren't you? Well, they're all here in the following eight "treasure chests." When you've completed a hunt and have all your answers, you may "unlock" the chests by tearing along the perforated edge. But no peeking until you're ready to see those answers!

What happens if you only want to see the answers for one land or one resort? A heading identifying each section appears before sets of questions. So just look for the appropriate heading and ignore any other answers. Quite frankly, the questions are printed small enough that you really need to be actively looking at them to read them (we did this on purpose, of course).

Because the font size is small on the answers, you may find it difficult to read the answers. If this is your dilemma, take a tip from the front cover of this book and use a magnifying glass. Oh, wait, you're standing in the middle of Main Street, U.S.A. without a magnifying glass? Ah, well, in that case, hand the book to the youngest member in your party to see if they can be of assistance. Better yet, try reading the type below now to see if it'll be a problem later—if you can't read it, find yourself a small magnifying glass and keep it with you. It'll come in handy when reading menus, too!

Sample Answers —This text is the smallest size that we use to display answers in the "treasure chests." It is 7.5-point type set in Myriad Pro Light Condensed. If you can read it unaided, good for you! If not, then you've either got yourself a magnifying glass or a younger person, so again, congratulations!

Now, we expect there will be a few hunters who disagree with our answers. That's why we always try to give the actual location of the answer in parentheses after it. This also gives you an opportunity to revisit the scene and look for those elusive answers. Of course, if you feel we've made a mistake or the answer no longer exists due to a change, please contact us with the information on page 157.

If you've opened the treasure hunts but want to close them again to discourage future peeking, just use tape along the edges.

Treasure Chest #1
Magic Kingdom

Open chest (tear perforation) to view the Magic Kingdom answers.

Answers to Magic Kingdom's Main Street, U.S.A. — **MS-1:** 10 cents (second floor of station); **MS-2:** Two (second floor of station); **MS-3:** Lincoln and Washington (on wall behind counter); **MS-4:** 1 (Braille map is located in City Hall); **MS-5:** W.D.W.F.D. (rear left of Firehouse); **MS-6:** Harmony Barber Shop (near the Firehouse in the Town Square); **MS-7:** 50 lbs (right rear of shop); **MS-8:** 1888 (painted on the facade); **MS-9:** One run (Scoreboard in Casey's Corner back seating area); **MS-10:** Carnation Good Start (beside Crystal Palace); **MS-11:** Crystal Palace (sign outside of Crystal Palace); **MS-12:** Paw prints (presumably the prints belong to the Lady and the Tramp); **MS-13:** Yes (Goofy is cast in bronze permanently outside Exposition Hall); **MS-14:** End of the alleyway (right side of Main Street breezeway); **MS-15:** Phil Harris (in the back of Exposition Hall on the mural showing the history of Walt Disney movies); **MS-16:** Larry Slocum (window near Plaza Inn); **MS-17:** Republic Field (scoreboard in Casey's Corner back seating area); **MS-18:** Distinctive Achievement (in the Back of Exposition Hall on the mural showing the history of Walt Disney movies); **MS-19:** Mud Kings (on sign over door of shop); **MS-20:** "If we can dream it, we can do it" (in a window above the store entrance in the Main Street Confectionery shop); **MS-21:** Mogul 2-6-0 (locomotive history display in the Main Street Train Station breezeway); **MS-22:** Royal (sign on the upper wall in the Marketplace, which is the first shop on the right after you pass the alley on Main Street, U.S.A.); **MS-23:** 1902 (banner in the Main Street Train Station waiting area); **MS-24:** Two bells (rear right wall of Firehouse); **MS-25:** Coca-Cola (wall sign at Casey's Corner near the seating area entrance); **MS-26:** Trip routing, tour books, and maps (kiosk is inside exposition hall); **MS-27:** 690 miles (mural in the Main Street Train Station waiting area); **MS-28:** Bacon's (bottle display in the Marketplace); **MS-29:** Buena Vista Magic Lanterns Slides (second floor window above Confectionery/Cinema boundary); **MS-30:** Dick Tunis (second story window above Main Street Bakery); **MS-31:** Bequerly's Stamp and Seal Orlando 841-8083 (second floor of Main Street Train Station); **MS-32:** 1895 (window on second floor of the alleyway halfway down Main Street); **MS-33:** G rolls (second floor of Main Street Train Station); **MS-34:** Shampoo (bottle display in the Marketplace); **MS-35:** Rawlings (boxes are to the right of the counter, along the Main Street Athletic Club wall); **MS-36:** S.S. Bedard (sign outside the Car Barn on Main Street)

Answers to Magic Kingdom's Adventureland — **AL-1:** Drums (seen atop Adventureland entrance sign on bridge and heard in background music); **AL-2:** The Swiss Family Robinson: husband, wife, and three sons Fritz, Francis, and Ernest (sign outside of the Swiss Family Treehouse); **AL-3:** Spitting at them (The Magic Carpets of Aladdin); **AL-4:** A paintbrush—Iago is holding a hammer (sign outside of Enchanted Tiki Room—Under New Management); **AL-5:** Shrunken Ned's Junior Jungle Boats (names of radio-controlled boats); **AL-6:** Four ships (on sign on corner of building); **AL-7:** Plants (fountain across from Pirates of the Caribbean); **AL-8:** It has holes in it (to the left of the entrance to Pirates of the Caribbean); **AL-9:** The pirate parrot (above the entrance to Pirates of the Caribbean); **AL-10:** A pirate and a parrot (across from Pirates of the Caribbean ride); **AL-11:** Spit water and play the sound of beating drums (near Jungle Cruise entrance); **AL-12:** July 17, 1805 (sign outside of the Swiss Family Treehouse); **AL-13:** They're attached to the plate (seen during Enchanted Tiki Room show); **AL-14:** Tales (beginning of Pirates of the Caribbean ride); **AL-15:** Men (in the Pirates Bazaar shop at the exit of Pirates of the Caribbean); **AL-16:** The "moron Tiki gods" (Zazu's response to Iago's question about the lights in the Enchanted Tiki Room show); **AL-17:** Six climbers (seen while riding the Jungle Cruise); **AL-18:** The drop (if you said two, you've been riding Disneyland's version too much and your memory is clouded); **AL-19:** Jose (seen while riding the Jungle Cruise); **AL-20:** Pyramid (right upper shelf of the Pirates of the Caribbean); **AL-21:** Michael, Jose, Pierre, and Fritz (heard during Enchanted Tiki Room show); **AL-22:** One tiger (seen while riding the Jungle Cruise); **AL-23:** Michael, Jose, Pierre, and Fritz (heard during Enchanted Tiki Room show); **AL-24:** 5:59 am (on sign on back wall, right side near the ceiling); **AL-25:** Chicken (Carlos is being dunked in the well on Pirates of the Caribbean); **AL-26:** Lard (seen while riding Pirates of the Caribbean); **AL-27:** Smelling salts (queue of Jungle Cruise); **AL-28:** 8 cannons (seen while riding Pirates of the Caribbean); **AL-29:** Chicken (menu is posted to the right of the Jungle Cruise FASTPASS machines); **AL-30:** E. L. O'Fevre (sign at Jungle Cruise exit); **AL-31:** New Delhi, India (sign at Jungle Cruise exit); **AL-32:** 1107 (sign by cash registers); **AL-33:** Anaheim (you may have to step way back to see it); **AL-34:** Iago heard just as the exit doors close after the Enchanted Tiki Room show; **AL-35:** On roof above bazaar near Aladdin's

Answers to Magic Kingdom's Frontierland — **FR-1:** Two rifles (sign on Frontierland Shootin' Arcade); **FR-2:** Red, white, and gray (an owl (on roof of Frontierland Shootin' Arcade)); **FR-3:** An owl (center of diorama at Frontierland Shootin' Arcade); **FR-4:** Texas (sign on Frontier Trading Post); **FR-5:** 1898 (sign above the entrance); **FR-6:** 1879 (painted at top of Pecos Bill Tall Tale Inn & Café); **FR-7:** Rivers of America (on quidemaps, signs); **FR-8:** Harper's Mill (visible while standing in Frontierland); **FR-9:** On Brer Bear's club (in front of Splash Mountain); **FR-10:** 1:20 (clock in Briar Patch shop near Splash Mountain exit); **FR-11:** Laughin' Place (on sign near Splash Mountain); **FR-12:** Near exit of Big Thunder Mountain (on sign); **FR-13:** A frown (Frontierland Shootin' Arcade); **FR-14:** Three mounts (inside theater); **FR-15:** Boots (Splash Mountain queue); **FR-16:** Pink (seen while riding big Thunder Mountain); **FR-17:** White star (on west wall of toppings bar area inside Pecos Bill Tall Tale Inn & Café); **FR-18:** B flat (mentioned in show); **FR-19:** Pink (seen at end of show); **FR-20:** Salt (seen while riding Splash Mountain); **FR-21:** Pink (seen on various statues near Splash Mountain, as well as on Splash Mountain itself); **FR-22:** Blue (lobby of Country Bear Jamboree); **FR-23:** Guitar (seen in show); **FR-24:** Brer Roadrunner (seen while riding Splash Mountain); **FR-25:** A carriage and harness repository (sign at Frontier Trading Post); **FR-26:** You see a "For Sale" sign (Frontierland Shootin' Arcade); **FR-27:** 35 heads (sign at Frontier Trading Post); **FR-28:** Caves (sign inside Country Bear Jamboree); **FR-29:** McGraw (mentioned during show); **FR-30:** Slue Foot Sue (far west seating area, northwest corner, inside Pecos Bill Tall Tale Inn & Café); **FR-31:** A funnel (visible in scene); **FR-32:** Muskrat (it's overlooking the castle); **FR-33:** Feb. 13 (on tombstone at Frontierland Shootin' Arcade—someone has to find the tombstone in order to view the date); **FR-34:** Hives (heard while riding Splash Mountain); **FR-35:** "Respect the Land, Defend the Defenseless . . . and don't ever spit in front of women and children!" (inside Pecos Bill Tall Tale Inn & Café); **FR-36:** "Ain't no place that far" (Splash Mountain queue); **FR-37:** Laugh (heard while riding Splash Mountain); **FR-38:** Old Betsy (back wall of Pecos Bill Tall Tale Inn & Café)

Answers to Magic Kingdom's Liberty Square — **LS-1:** 10; **LS-2:** 14 flags (near the Liberty Tree); **LS-3:** Yes (near the Liberty Tree); **LS-4:** Smuckers (sign on Yankee Traders); **LS-5:** 1777, which is the year that it's exactly 200 Years before the Magic Kingdom opened); **LS-6:** Twenty lanterns (sign on Liberty Tree Tavern); **LS-7:** Four men (sign on Columbia Harbour House); **LS-8:** Mickey shape (painted on side of riverboat, on signs, on guidemaps); **LS-9:** Liberty Belle (painted on side of riverboat); **LS-10:** Ye Olde Christmas Shoppe; **LS-11:** Two candles (seen on outside wall); **LS-12:** Two ghosts (seen at exit of The Haunted Mansion); **LS-13:** Three ghosts (seen at exit of The Haunted Mansion); **LS-14:** Music and voice (sign seen outside Ye Olde Christmas Shoppe); **LS-15:** Master Gracey (on tombstone in front of The Haunted Mansion); **LS-16:** Chief Justice Marshall (sign in Liberty Bell area); **LS-17:** White Towers (seen on The Haunted Mansion); **LS-18:** A big rock (on tombstone on The Haunted Mansion); **LS-19:** A spider (seen on The Haunted Mansion); **LS-20:** Georgia (sign in Liberty Bell area); **LS-21:** 1787 which also happens to be the year the constitution was ratified (numbers on top of building that houses the Hall of Presidents); **LS-22:** 1898 (seen near outside The Haunted Mansion); **LS-23:** a new nation waiting to be born (Welcome to Liberty Square sign); **LS-24:** Madame Leota (on cart outside The Haunted Mansion); **LS-25:** "I Saw Three Ships" (near register of Ye Olde Christmas Shoppe); **LS-26:** five ghosts (seen on The Haunted Mansion); **LS-27:** An axe (on tombstone in The Haunted Mansion); **LS-28:** Green (seen at start of The Haunted Mansion); **LS-29:** A cabin on the bank (seen while riding the Liberty Square Riverboat); **LS-30:** Lucretia (exit of The Hall of Presidents); **LS-31:** Southern Live Oak/ Quercus Virginiana (sign near tree); **LS-32:** Cherry (lamp above Madame Leota in the seance room of Haunted Mansion); **LS-33:** Red (seen while riding Haunted Mansion); **LS-34:** Ben Franklin (seen at exit of The Hall of Presidents); **LS-35:** WED-TV (seen during the Hall of Presidents)

Answers to Magic Kingdom's Fantasyland — **FL-1:** Green with envy and red with anger (in mural in the breezeway through Cinderella Castle); **FL-2:** Her crown, and if you curtsy to her the crown will appear to be on her head (the fountain is behind Cinderella Castle, near Tinker Bell's Treasures shop); **FL-3:** Sir Mickey's (behind Cinderella Castle); **FL-4:** Sword Shaped (south of Cinderella's Golden Carousel); **FL-5:** Purple (seen from walkway near Cinderella's Golden Carousel); **FL-6:** Coach mice from Cinderella (top of sign); **FL-7:** Red horse #7 on Cinderella's Golden Carousel); **FL-8:** Seven (on "Seven Dwarfs Mine" sign above Snow White's Scary Adventures); **FL-9:** Red (seen while riding The Many Adventures of Winnie the Pooh); **FL-10:** Tigger (sign for The Many Adventures of Winnie the Pooh); **FL-11:** Hanging out of Mr. Sanders Tree (Pooh's Playful Spot); **FL-12:** The top of the teapot in the center (Mad Tea Party); **FL-13:** Belle (guidemaps, seen during shows); **FL-14:** "Your wishes will help the dreams of children come true" (the Wishing Well is between Cinderella Castle and the Fairytale Garden); **FL-15:** A Candle (seen while riding Snow White's Scary Adventures); **FL-16:** A Rabbit (seen while riding Snow White's Scary Adventures); **FL-17:** Jasmine (seen during the magic carpet scene of Mickey's PhilharMagic); **FL-18:** Cleo, Figaro, Jiminy Cricket, Blue Fairy, Monstro, Geppetto's Workshop, and surprise! (painted on walls of dining areas in The Pinocchio Village Haus); **FL-19:** Chapter 11 (seen while riding The Many Adventures of Winnie the Pooh); **FL-20:** Donald Duck (heard at beginning of Mickey's PhilharMagic); **FL-21:** White and red (visible from walkway near Peter Pan's Flight); **FL-22:** Jigger—big surprise! (seen while riding The Many Adventures of Winnie the Pooh); **FL-23:** Two buzzards (seen while riding Snow White's Scary Adventures); **FL-24:** Three mermaids (seen while riding Peter Pan's Flight); **FL-25:** Yellow (seen during the Be Our Guest scene of Mickey's PhilharMagic); **FL-26:** Blue (seen while riding Peter Pan's Flight); **FL-27:** 1:45, give or take a few minutes (seen while riding Peter Pan's Flight); **FL-28:** A cowboy and an eskimo (seen toward end of It's a small world"); **FL-29:** A dog (seen while riding Peter Pan's Flight); **FL-30:** The play fountain in Pooh's Playful Spot (sign at Pooh's Playful Spot); **FL-31:** Tinker Bell (dresser is in south end of shop, nearest to the castle); **FL-32:** A buffalo (seen while riding the Many Adventures of Winnie the Pooh); **FL-33:** A piano (seen during Mickey's PhilharMagic); **FL-34:** Hunny (seen while riding the Many Adventures of Winnie the Pooh); **FL-35:** Mickey's PhilharMagic (sign above Mickey's PhilharMagic); **FL-36:** Humpty (seen while riding Peter Pan's Flight); **FL-37:** Mickey Mouse March (seen during the first scene of Mickey's PhilharMagic); **FL-38:** Peddler's Disguise (seen during Snow White's Scary Adventures); **FL-39:** Please check armour at the door (window of Sir Mickey shop behind Cinderella Castle); **FL-40:** Raggedy Ann and Andy (seen at the initial lift point of Peter Pan's Flight);

Answers to Magic Kingdom's Mickey's Toontown Fair — **TT-1:** Mickey Mouse (Mickey's Toontown Fair entrance sign); **TT-2:** A wrench (sign above Pete's Garage); **TT-3:** The keys to the restroom in front of Pete's Garage — note that the Gas Gulp Pump is sometimes "off" and the keys may not be noticeable (sign in front of Pete's Garage); **TT-4:** 2N TWN FR for Toon Town (sign in front of Pete's Garage); **TT-5:** Silver, red, green, and blue (behind Pete's Garage); **TT-6:** A propeller (in front of The Barnstormer at Goofy's Wiseacre Farm); **TT-7:** Red (top of Mickey's Country House); **TT-8:** Cornelius Coot (scroll near statue in front of Toontown Hall of Fame tent); **TT-9:** Donald Duck (Donald's Boat); **TT-10:** Yellow Mickey heads (sign on Toontown Train Station); **TT-11:** Toon Park (in front of little house in Toon Park); **TT-12:** Pete (painted to the right of the doors on Pete's Garage); **TT-13:** "Good to the Last Toon" (Minnie's Country House); **TT-14:** Goofey Tech and Duckberg U (Minnie's Country House); **TT-15:** Quack Sea (Donald's Boat); **TT-16:** Awful hot, volcanic hot, very hot, hot (Minnie's Country House); **TT-17:** S.S. Daisy (painted on Donald's Boat); **TT-18:** No. 2 (Minnie's Country House); **TT-19:** "Give Your Face a toon-up" (sign on awning of Pete's Paint Shop); **TT-20:** 6 (Mickey's Country House); **TT-21:** MIK MIN (hanging on the wall in Mickey's shed behind Mickey's Country House); **TT-22:** Mickey (game room of Mickey's Country House); **TT-23:** Pink (studio of Mickey's Country House); **TT-24:** Red Barns (W-A-C-K-Y Radio near The Barnstormer at Goofy's Wiseacre Farm); **TT-25:** MIK MIN (Minnie's Country House); **TT-26:** Dubious (The Barnstormer at Goofy's Wiseacre Farm); **TT-27:** Tail spin, rollover doughnut (The Barnstormer at Goofy's Wiseacre Farm); **TT-28:** MouseKoshi (in garden of Mickey's Country House); **TT-29:** Popcorn, squash, and peppers (barn at The Barnstormer at Goofy's Wiseacre Farm); **TT-30:** Florence Micingale (Minnie's Country House); **TT-31:** Drew the map (in cabin of Donald's Boat); **TT-32:** On plans for Mickey's automatic dishwasher (kitchen of Mickey's Country House); **TT-33:** Milo Mouse and Madeline VonMouse (photos on the living room wall of Minnie's Country House); **TT-34:** Peter Pan, Buzz Lightyear, Ariel, and Woody (near front door of Mickey's Country House); **TT-35:** A young Mickey Mouse (photo in bedroom of Mickey's Country House); **TT-36:** Minnie's back porch (rear of Minnie's Country House); **TT-37:** Cheesecake (on wall in queue); **TT-38:** Barnstormer at Goofy's Wiseacre Farm (on wall in queue);

Answers to Magic Kingdom's Tomorrowland — **TO-1:** Generating a Bright New Tomorrow (over entrance to Tomorrowland Arcade); **TO-2:** Avenue of the Planets (signs for the street can be found at the entrance to Tomorrowland); **TO-3:** Stitch's Great Escape (across from Buzz Lightyear's Space Ranger Spin); **TO-4:** Green (can be seen from ground); **TO-5:** Buzz Lightyear and Zurg (sign over entrance to Buzz Lightyear's Space Ranger Spin); **TO-6:** Blue (found near the Lunching Pad, and the Astro Orbiter elevators); **TO-7:** Three (one cog displays the current year, another Walt Disney's name and the initial of that attraction name); **TO-8:** Intercept Progress (located at Thirst Rangers soda stand); **TO-9:** Four lanes (can be seen from Grandstand area); **TO-10:** 1 (painted on front end of Indy car); **TO-11:** 33 (Tomorrowland Indy Speedway); **TO-12:** Across from Stitch's Great Escape (sign on building); **TO-13:** 1920s (seen while viewing Carousel of Progress); **TO-14:** 2 and Up (found throughout Buzz Lightyear's Space Ranger Spin); **TO-15:** 626 (seen and heard at Stitch's Great Escape); **TO-16:** A Cat (seen while viewing Carousel of Progress); **TO-17:** An adventure (heard while riding Tomorrowland Transit Authority); **TO-18:** Astro (seen while riding Buzz Lightyear's Space Ranger Spin); **TO-19:** Blue Line (visible from walkway underneath); **TO-20:** Chances are Good (on the floor near the Buzz Lightyear Audio-Animatronics); **TO-21:** Channel D (seen while riding Tomorrowland Transit Authority); **TO-22:** Dannmall X1 (Buzz Lightyear's Space Ranger Spin queue); **TO-23:** Galactic Gobblers (menu at the Lunching Pad); **TO-24:** Dannmall X1 (end of Stitch's Great Escape); **TO-25:** "Give them a mind... this bad pun can be heard as you approach the Carousel of Progress on the Tomorrowland Transit Authority); **TO-26:** Eleven (the aliens are on top of a small kiosk); **TO-27:** John's Chinese Restaurant (seen while viewing Carousel of Progress); **TO-28:** Six (Buzz Lightyear's Space Ranger Spin queue); **TO-29:** XP-37 (instruction sign in Buzz Lightyear's Space Ranger Spin queue); **TO-30:** Six (in front of Space Mountain); **TO-31:** Root Beer (seen while viewing Carousel of Progress); **TO-32:** Space Mountain (narrator makes the announcement just as you enter Space Mountain); **TO-33:** Rover (seen and heard at Stitch's Great Escape); **TO-34:** Stitch is a level 3 prisoner (seen and heard at Stitch's Great Escape); **TO-35:** Rover (Zurg's secret weapon, which appears twice in Buzz Lightyear's Space Ranger Spin); **TO-36:** Two on the lift hill and can be seen from Space Mountain and the Tomorrowland Transit Authority); **TO-37:** Red (Zurg's secret weapon, seen in Buzz Lightyear's Space Ranger Spin); **TO-38:** Marty (note is on the board over the desk at the extreme right of the final scene); **TO-39:** Third (Zurg's secret weapon appears twice in Buzz Lightyear's Space Ranger Spin); **TO-40:** An atmosphere with 15 lb/in squared pressure (heard on the delivery boxes at the Thirst Rangers soda stand); **TO-41:** Disney's Hilton Head resort (alien statue near Disney Vacation Club kiosk near Auntie Gravity's); **TO-42:** Your hair display in the Buzz Lightyear's Space Ranger Spin portion of the Tomorrowland Transit Authority); **TO-43:** The Great Majestic (seen while viewing Carousel of Progress); **TO-44:** A time machine (narrator of the Tomorrowland Transit Authority makes the announcement as you near the station at Rockettower Plaza); **TO-45:** The Tomorrowland Transit Authority Blue Line (an announcement is heard between Space Mountain and Carousel of Progress on the Tomorrowland Transit Authority); **TO-46:** Gravity and Antigravity (poster on the walkway between Avenue of the Planets and Tomorrowland Terrace Noodle Station); **TO-47:** PUSH, the walking trash can (wanders around Tomorrowland, particularly near Cosmic Ray's Starlight Cafe)

Answers to Photos Under the Treasure Chest — **MK-A:** In front of Peter Pan's Flight (Fantasyland); **MK-B:** On top of Mickey's PhilharMagic (Fantasyland); **MK-C:** In Barnstormer queue (Mickey's Toontown Fair); **MK-D:** On top of Tomorrowland Arcade (Tomorrowland); **MK-E:** Behind Hall of Presidents (Liberty Square)

Under the Treasure Chest

Where in the Magic Kingdom can you find these five images?

(Answers are inside the treasure chest, of course!)

MK-A

MK-B

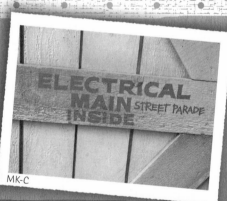

MK-C

MK-D

MK-E

Treasure Chest #2
Epcot

Open chest (tear perforation) to view the Epcot answers.

Answers to Epcot's Future World East — **FE-1:** Get your photo taken at the Leave a Legacy sales area (west side of the entrance plaza); **FE-2:** Disney Hand (sign on fountain in entrance plaza); **FE-3:** Spaceship Earth (guidemaps; signs); **FE-4:** The history of human communications (signs outside Spaceship Earth); **FE-5:** Tomorrow (sign on Innovations); **FE-6:** Every 15 minutes during park hours (time it, or you may find it mentioned in a guidemap); **FE-7:** Trojan Battery Co. (Solar Bench at the exit of Innovations East); **FE-8:** Dinosaurs, extra credit if you wrote Tyrannosaurus, Stegosaurus, and Sauropod (in front of and beside Universe of Energy); **FE-9:** Red (Jupiter in the middle of Mission:SPACE entry plaza); **FE-10:** Kalpana Chawla (quote plaque nearest the entrance to Mission:SPACE); **FE-11:** Four (inside the big planet at Mission:SPACE entrance); **FE-12:** Triton and Orion (Mission:SPACE entrance); **FE-13:** Space (Postcards From Space booth in post-show exhibits, which you can enter through gift shop without first riding); **FE-14:** Space Base (post-show area of Mission:SPACE, also mentioned on guidemaps); **FE-15:** They are in the shape of Mickey (on wall at Mission:SPACE Cargo Bay shop); **FE-16:** Drinking a Coke (Cool Wash is near last Track); **FE-17:** 3:30 (sign outside last Track); **FE-18:** "Warning, you're no dummy" (warning signs outside last Track, which you can enter through gift shop if you aren't riding); **FE-19:** Cadillac (post-show area of last Track); **FE-20:** Butterfly Chrysalises (near MouseGear and Cool Wash); **FE-21:** 115.0 meters/378.2 feet (large display in Mission:SPACE queue); **FE-22:** 1924 (large display in Mission:SPACE queue); **FE-23:** 2036 (sign at last Track, viewed during last Track); **FE-24:** 23 (mentioned during last Track); **FE-25:** The north polar cap of Mars (pre-boarding brief video for Mission:SPACE); **FE-26:** 6500 Tons (just past the photo booth on the right hand side as you exit last Track); **FE-27:** Alexi Leonov (on photo wall of Mission:SPACE); **FE-28:** Mesa, AZ (photograph in last Track pre-show area); **FE-29:** 1997 (numerous references throughout last Track); **FE-30:** Sunspot (on photo wall of Mission:SPACE); **FE-31:** The beginning of our tomorrow" (poster outside the Spaceship Earth entrance); **FE-32:** KRNG (Get It? Energy, Yeah, it's silly) (seen during Ellen's Energy Adventure); **FE-33:** Plain and Galvanized (sign in last Track queue); **FE-34:** Lieutenant (pre-show video for Mission:SPACE); **FE-35:** The roads (heard during Spaceship Earth); **FE-36:** 1 and 1/16th (Cool Wash near last Track exit); **FE-37:** Six (road signs at last Track exit); **FE-38:** 29 markers, representing the 29 missions between 1959 and 1976 (entry plaza of Mission:SPACE); **FE-39:** To allow mobility-impaired guests to board (sign at the entrance to the load area of Spaceship Earth); **FE-40:** Aerospike Engine (large display in Mission:SPACE queue); **FE-41:** Corrosives (seen during last Track); **FE-42:** Sleeping (seen during Spaceship Earth); **FE-43:** Six (seen during Mission:SPACE queue); **FE-44:** Six (seen at end of last Track); **FE-45:** Phoenecians (heard during Spaceship Earth); **FE-46:** X-2 Engineer (mentioned during Mission:SPACE); **FE-47:** 2 1/2 tons (seen during last Track); **FE-48:** 26.4 (display in last Track pre-show); **FE-49:** Nov 21, 2035 (wall 7'6" loading area of last Track); **FE-50:** 26.4 (display in last Track pre-show); **FE-51:** 8.7 MPH (Mission:SPACE queue); **FE-52:** A man with a beard—he is Dave Marx, the husband of the editor of this guide, Jennifer Marx (Leave a Legacy monument—west side, sixth monument, column A, third plaque, 10 images up, and eight images from the left); **FE-53:** A rock shaped like a turkey leg (mural at the top of the entrance ramp to Spaceship Earth); **FE-54:** Brain Power (final Jeopardy Question in Ellen's Energy Adventure pre-show); **FE-55:** "MOO" (seen during last Track); **FE-56:** Nine (pre-boarding brief video for Mission:SPACE); **FE-57:** Solid Hydrogen (pre-boarding brief video of Mission:SPACE); **FE-58:** Princeton (heard during Ellen's Energy Adventure pre-show); **FE-59:** Red (sign behind the Mission Control desks in Mission:SPACE queue); **FE-60:** Snap On (last Track queue); **FE-61:** A rock shaped like a turkey leg (mural at top of entrance ramp to Spaceship Earth); **FE-62:** Styrofoam (last Track queue); **FE-63:** Jerry (seen during Spaceship Earth); **FE-64:** The Atlantic (seen during Spaceship Earth); **FE-65:** "The exploration of deep space" (pre-boarding brief video of Mission:SPACE); **FE-66:** The New York Daily (seen during Spaceship Earth); **FE-67:** Think Safety (seen during last Track); **FE-68:** WDP (seen during Spaceship Earth); **FE-69:** The Corvette (sign outside of last Track); **FE-70:** Innovations East (near House of Innovations)

Answers to Epcot's Future World West — **FW-1:** Lutron (sign at exhibit); **FW-2:** Balzac (kiosk in breezeway); **FW-3:** Inventor's Circle (set into pavement, west of Innovations); **FW-4:** It talks! (the talking drinking fountain is near the restrooms); **FW-5:** Finding Nemo (in front of The Living Seas); **FW-6:** Seven—Dory, Marlin, Nemo, Pearl, Gil and Bloat (in front of The Living Seas); **FW-7:** It has crashing waves (painted on side of pylon in front of The Living Seas); **FW-8:** The Living Seas (guidemaps; signs); **FW-9:** Nestle (sign at front of pavilion); **FW-10:** Four balloons—the fifth sphere is the planet earth (suspended from ceiling in The Land); **FW-11:** Planet Earth (suspended from ceiling in The Land); **FW-12:** A sunflower (second floor of The Land); **FW-13:** At the Nestle Junior Chef program near Sunshine Seasons eatery (in The Land pavilion); **FW-14:** Journey Into Imagination (in front of pavilion); **FW-15:** Purple—it's Figment the dragon (in front of Imagination pavilion); **FW-16:** Kodak (sign at front of pavilion); **FW-17:** Yellow and red (various locations on and off Journey Into Imagination—his shirt matches the corporate colors of the attraction's sponsor, Kodak); **FW-18:** In front of the Imagination pavilion (on the character's image); **FW-19:** 3 rows (seen on Bruce replica in Bruce's Sub House); **FW-20:** 25 (Celsius or 77 Fahrenheit (sign in the observation area of The Living Seas); **FW-21:** 3 (noted on Submouseable); **FW-22:** Bugs in a Bun (seen during "Circle of Life" movie); **FW-23:** Mr. Ray's Lagoon (lower level of The Living Seas pavilion); **FW-24:** By waving your hands in the air (ImageWorks is the post-show after Journey Into Imagination); **FW-25:** California (seen while riding Soarin'); **FW-26:** Chicken (first scene of Journey Into Imagination); **FW-27:** Disneyland in California (seen while watching "Honey, I Shrunk the Audience"); **FW-28:** Dr. Wayne Szalinski (heard while watching "Honey, I Shrunk the Audience"); **FW-29:** Manager of Everything Else (Journey Into Imagination queue); **FW-30:** Figment Pigment (seen while riding Journey Into Imagination); **FW-31:** Gigabyte (heard while riding Soarin'); **FW-32:** Hans Christian Andersen (wall of quotes near the entrance to the Living With the Land boat ride); **FW-33:** Horse Droppings (heard during "Circle of Life" movie); **FW-34:** Hot Apple Pie (in the smell canister on the floor, seen while riding Journey Into Imagination); **FW-35:** Mice (felt during the mice duplication scene in "Honey, I Shrunk the Audience"); **FW-36:** Photon (heard while watching "Honey, I Shrunk the Audience"); **FW-37:** Rainforest (heard during Living With the Land); **FW-38:** Royal Gramma (display in The Living Seas); **FW-39:** The balloon is a lightbulb with little wings (seen during Journey Into Imagination); **FW-40:** Three (seen while riding Journey Into Imagination); **FW-41:** Level Two of The Living Seas pavilion (seen while riding Journey Into Imagination); **FW-42:** Timon and Pumbaa (seen during "Circle of Life" movie); **FW-43:** Yellow (second scene of Journey Into Imagination); **FW-44:** 1543 (noted on Innovations breezeway); **FW-45:** 1987 (sign in the observation area of The Living Seas); **FW-46:** 82 (prairie scene in the Living With the Land boat ride); **FW-47:** Bruce's Sub House (in The Living Seas pavilion); **FW-48:** Butterfly fish (on display in The Living Seas pavilion); **FW-49:** Mickey Mouse (seen during the golfing scene—look fast, its only on the screen for half a second); **FW-50:** Coral Reef (in The Living Seas pavilion); **FW-51:** The Wet Look (heard during "Circle of Life" movie); **FW-52:** The air (said by Timon in the "Circle of Life" film); **FW-53:** The Golden Gate Bridge (seen while riding Soarin'); **FW-54:** Yellow (upside down scene in Journey Into Imagination); **FW-55:** A kind of fish, like Gill from "Finding Nemo" (on display in The Living Seas); **FW-56:** Tickle Testing (door on the right of your vehicle as you exit the Smell Lab area of Journey Into Imagination, also known as Journey Into Imagination With Figment); **FW-57:** Visual Confusion in sight testing lab of the Imagination Institute (in sight testing lab of the Imagination Institute, also known as Journey Into Imagination With Figment); **FW-58:** Yellow (upside down scene in Journey Into Imagination); **FW-59:** Green—It's the birthstone of the eldest son of the family who created the murals (located on the right rear, about 3 feet from the door and approximately 6 feet off the ground); **FW-60:** In front of Innovations West (it's the back of the Innovations sign)

Answers to Epcot's World Showcase East — **WE-1:** Family meal with food and bowls (display of moden Mexican home inside Mexico pavilion); **WE-2:** Inside Mexico pavilion (on signs and guidemaps); **WE-3:** San Angel Inn (inside Mexico pavilion); **WE-4:** Two mailboxes (between Mexico and Norway); **WE-5:** 14 — 10 small dragsonils and 4 large dragon heads (Norway pavilion); **WE-6:** Sod, or grass (on seating area roof at Norway); **WE-7:** Red and white (Norway pavilion); **WE-8:** Eight fingers and eight toes (The Puffin's Roost store in Norway); **WE-9:** Coke (between China and Germany); **WE-10:** Four (front of China pavilion); **WE-11:** Six (flags in China pavilion, guidemaps); **WE-12:** Lisu (map in "Land of Many Faces" exhibition near Reflections of China); **WE-13:** A dragon (Germany pavilion); **WE-14:** A bell (Germany); **WE-15:** Red (toy shop in Germany); **WE-16:** Model trains (between Germany and Italy); **WE-17:** In the water (in front of Italy); **WE-18:** Fish (columned shop in Italy); **WE-19:** Bowling balls (columned shop in Italy); **WE-20:** Red Cross (Italy); **WE-21:** The glockenspiel clock (in the Germany pavilion); **WE-22:** 100,000 (heard during "Reflections of China" movie); **WE-23:** 1692 (sign on quick-service eatery in Mexico); **WE-24:** 28 (sign in the Stave Church in Norway); **WE-25:** A triton shell (fountain in Italy); **WE-26:** Triangle circle triangle (columned shop in Italy); **WE-27:** As the clock strikes the bell, two Hummel figurines come out — It's like the famous Glockenspiel in Munich (toy shop in Germany); **WE-28:** Blue-green (toy shop in Germany); **WE-29:** Bounty, prosperity, and fertility (seen during El Rio del Tiempo ride in Mexico); **WE-30:** Torches (seen during El Rio del Tiempo ride in Mexico); **WE-31:** Three trolls (seen while riding Maelstrom); **WE-32:** Herzlich Willkommen (mural in back of "Sommerfest" of Germany pavilion); **WE-33:** Hotel Casa Grande (seen during El Rio del Tiempo ride in Mexico); **WE-34:** Kola (between China and Germany); **WE-35:** Miao, Yi, Maonqolia, and Naxi (display in "Land of Many Faces" exhibition near Reflections of China); **WE-36:** N80 08N (mural behind boarding area of Maelstrom); **WE-37:** Norst Dare (above theater entrance near Reflections of China); **WE-38:** Red symbolizes happiness (display in "Land of Many Faces" exhibition near Reflections of China); **WE-39:** Royal Cruise Line, Royal Viking Line, and Norwegian Cruise Line (seen after riding Maelstrom); **WE-40:** Seven (seen during "Reflections of China" movie); **WE-41:** Star shaped (seen during El Rio del Tiempo ride in Mexico); **WE-42:** The Cosmos (display in "Land of Many Faces" exhibition near Reflections of China); **WE-43:** The Olympics (sign in the Stave Church in Norway); **WE-44:** The Silk Road (mentioned during "Reflections of China" movie); **WE-45:** Three ballerinas (seen during "Norway — The Movie" after riding Maelstrom); **WE-46:** Three million (display in "Land of Many Faces" exhibition near Reflections of China); **WE-47:** Three polar bears (seen while riding Maelstrom); **WE-48:** 3 Jun 88 (seen on sign after exiting Maelstrom movie theater — it is on the right side before entering the store); **WE-49:** Atomic (seen during "Norway — The Movie" after riding Maelstrom); **WE-50:** Authority (heard during "Reflections of China" movie); **WE-51:** Borge Ousland (seen on sign after exiting Maelstrom movie theater and before entering the store); **WE-52:** Chatillon (between China and Germany); **WE-53:** Dong jing (display in "Land of Many Faces" exhibition near Reflections of China); **WE-54:** Five snowshoes (sign at entrance to the store from the Maelstrom movie theater); **WE-55:** Four dancers (seen during El Rio del Tiempo ride in Mexico); **WE-56:** Gold/red striped, blue with white top, and a blue speaker pole (in water in front of Italy); **WE-57:** Helly Juell Hansen (sign at entrance to the store from the Maelstrom movie theater); **WE-58:** Heng Yuan Xiang (seen during "Reflections of China" movie); **WE-59:** Inspire the Next (sign in Japan Gallery exhibition); **WE-60:** In Cantina de San Angel (it's the name of the fountain on the south side of the Catina); **WE-61:** Nine — a lucky number (floor of building you enter to see Reflections of China); **WE-62:** Paal Helge Haugen (sign in the Stave Church in Norway); **WE-63:** R24K (seen during "Norway — The Movie" after riding Maelstrom); **WE-64:** Red (seen during El Rio del Tiempo ride in Mexico); **WE-65:** Riga (between China and Germany); **WE-66:** Three — they are Hapsburng Emperors (on second story facade of Das Kaufhaus shop in Germany); **WE-67:** Water (heard during Reflections of China movie); **WE-68:** on wall of Mexican house (on left as you enter the Mexico pavilion)

Answers to Epcot's World Showcase West — **WW-1:** Canada, Japan, Morocco, and the United Kingdom (between Showcase Plaza and Canada); **WW-2:** Seven (three outside Northwest Mercantile, four inside); **WW-3:** A keg of explosives (Trading Post and Northwest Mercantile in Canada); **WW-4:** Mounted Mickey (shop inside Northwest Mercantile shop in Canada); **WW-5:** Otium Cum Dignitate, which means Leisure With Dignity (sign on Rose and Crown Pub); **WW-6:** 1920 (sign on fish shop in United Kingdom); **WW-7:** Three (shop near back of U.K. pavilion); **WW-8:** Beside the canal (between France and U.K.); **WW-9:** Beauty & the Beast (in Plume et Palette shop in France pavilion); **WW-10:** Vins de Pays, which means country wine (restaurant in France); **WW-11:** Green (rooftops of Morocco); **WW-12:** Gate (signs left and right of first arch in Morocco); **WW-13:** Enameled (Gallery of Arts and History in Morocco); **WW-14:** Red (Gallery of Arts and History in Morocco); **WW-15:** Red (torn gate in Japan); **WW-16:** The bamboo fountain, or kakei, as it rises and falls (garden in Japan); **WW-17:** Two (bridge leading to Japan Gallery in Japan); **WW-18:** III — using III instead of IV was typical in Colonial America (near the top of the building that houses The American Adventure show); **WW-19:** Heritage Manor Gifts (U.S.A. pavilion); **WW-20:** Live oysters on pearls for sale (Mitsukoshi Department Store in Japan pavilion); **WW-21:** 100 Aker Woods West (enter behind the desk with a type writer in the Toy Soldier Shop in United Kingdom); **WW-22:** 17 days (heard during The American Adventure show); **WW-23:** 25,000 (seen during "O Canada!" film); **WW-24:** 32 (seen during "O Canada!" film); **WW-25:** 35 La Promenade (le Quai) (sign outside La Signature shop in France); **WW-26:** 83 feet (temple outside the Japan building); **WW-27:** A Donkey Ride (shop in United Kingdom); **WW-28:** British Columbia (sign in garden outside of Le Cellier Steakhouse in Canada); **WW-29:** Elegant Age worthy Chardonnay and Pinot Noir (La Cave à Vin à La Maison du Vin wine shop in France); **WW-30:** Four (seen during "O Canada!" film); **WW-31:** Iron Ball and Lasso (The American Adventure show); **WW-32:** Ichigo-ya (signs to right of first arch in Japan); **WW-33:** late 1930s (in toys exhibit in back half of the Plume Et Palette perfume shop in France); **WW-34:** Les Miserables (seen during "O Canada!" film); **WW-35:** Mr. Brady (heard during The American Adventure show); **WW-36:** One (seen during The American Adventure show); **WW-37:** Ontario (mentioned during "O Canada!" film); **WW-38:** Passion (heard during The American Adventure show); **WW-39:** rear back door of Toy Soldier shop (the package is on a bench); **WW-40:** Saddle and Lasso (The American Adventure theater); **WW-41:** Seven doors (four entrances and three exits); **WW-42:** Spirit of Knowledge (movie poster inside The American Adventure listing the cast); **WW-43:** Statue of Liberty (movie poster inside The American Adventure theater); **WW-44:** #105 (between France and U.K.); **WW-45:** 1643 Anno Domini (wine shop in France); **WW-46:** 18 degrees (seen during O Canada!); **WW-47:** 2 shillings (middle of the Toy Soldier shop in United Kingdom); **WW-48:** 48th century (sign in Mitsukoshi Store in Japan); **WW-49:** Atlantic HS (Japan Gallery in Japan); **WW-50:** Calgary Stampede (seen during "O Canada!" film); **WW-51:** Capt. Eddie Rickenbacker (seen during the American Adventure); **WW-52:** John Steinbeck (heard during The American Adventure show); **WW-53:** Katie Nanna (on book in back of the Toy Soldier shop in United Kingdom); **WW-54:** King George III (heard during The American Adventure show); **WW-55:** Marrakesh (sign to right of Bab gate at base of Minaret tower in Morocco); **WW-56:** Modest (heard during The American Adventure show); **WW-57:** New York Times (seen during The American Adventure show); **WW-58:** Overindulged in Philadelphia's fine food and drink (heard during The American Adventure show); **WW-59:** Palais Du Cinema (sign on building in France); **WW-60:** Talley-Ho horse-drawn sightseeing (seen during "O Canada!" film); **WW-61:** The Navy (heard during The American Adventure show)

Answers to Photos Under the Treasure Chest — **EP-A:** In "window" inside MouseGear (Future World East); **EP-B:** Near ceiling in Northwest Mercantile (Canada); **EP-C:** On wall in Liberty Inn (American Adventure pavilion); **EP-D:** On shore in front of Mexico pavilion (World Showcase); **EP-E:** Suspended from ceiling in The Land (Future World West)

Under the Treasure Chest

Where in Epcot can you find these five images?

(Answers are inside the treasure chest, of course!)

EP-A

EP-B

EP-C

EP-D

EP-E

Treasure Chest #3
Disney–MGM Studios™

Open chest (tear perforation) to view the Studios answers.

Answers to Disney-MGM Studios' Hollywood Boulevard

HB-1: A globe (above Crossroads of the World kiosk in entry plaza); **HB-2:** 2158 miles (signpost outside Sid Cahuenga's One-of-a-Kind shop); **HB-4:** 1928, same year that Mickey was "born" (sign above L.A. Prop Cinema Storage shop); **HB-5:** The Darkroom (sign on photo shop); **HB-6:** 216 (sign outside shop); **HB-7:** Nestle Toll House (sign above the Starring Rolls Bakery); **HB-8:** Six brooms (in front of The Hollywood Brown Derby restaurant); **HB-9:** 606 7/8 (sign inside hat—look up!); **HB-10:** Noseprint (in front of The Great Movie Ride); **HB-11:** 12 spaces (The Great Movie Ride queue); **HB-12:** 1928 (sign at the entrance of The Hollywood Brown Derby restaurant); **HB-13:** 8/28/89 (in courtyard of The Great Movie Ride); **HB-14:** A sword and a monkey head (The Great Movie Ride queue); **HB-15:** Ambassador (lobby of The Great Movie Ride); **HB-16:** Red (seen while riding The Great Movie Ride); **HB-17:** Banana Company (sign on guidemaps); **HB-18:** Billy Joel (in courtyard of The Great Movie Ride); **HB-19:** Florida Hospital (sign near first aid station at front of park); **HB-20:** Handprints—he claims they are footprints (in courtyard of The Great Movie Ride); **HB-21:** Hollywood and Vine (seen while boarding The Great Movie Ride); **HB-22:** Mount Hollywood Art School (seen while riding The Great Movie Ride); **HB-23:** Rome (signpost in front of Sid's Cahuenga's store near entrance to park); **HB-24:** Red Oak Social Club (seen while riding the Alien scene while riding The Great Movie Ride); **HB-25:** Sigourney Weaver (heard as you enter the Alien scene while riding The Great Movie Ride); **HB-26:** Thirteen (seen while riding The Great Movie Ride); **HB-27:** Thousands (seen while boarding The Great Movie Ride); **HB-28:** Earffel Tower—a water tower with Mickey ears that used to be the Studios' park icon (seen from certain vantage points in and out of the park); **HB-29:** When engines running, oil or gas lights burning, or occupants are smoking (sign at the stroller rental area); **HB-30:** 021429 (seen while riding The Great Movie Ride); **HB-31:** 1000 miles (map on the back side of the Disney-MGM Studios tip board); **HB-32:** Thirteen (near Sid Cahuenga's store); **HB-33:** Hugo Bark (above the Pluto Toy Palace sign); **HB-34:** Hollywoodland (billboard above the Dark Room camera shop); **HB-36:** Jon (near Sid Cahuenga's store); **HB-37:** Justin Stitches (window above the Hollywood Fashion store); **HB-38:** Man or Beast (sign by the Dentist in the Western scene on The Great Movie Ride); **HB-39:** Packard 27777 (sign in the window above Cover Story shop); **HB-40:** Patrick J. Ryan's Bar (seen while riding The Great Movie Ride); **HB-41:** Service de Nuit (seen while riding The Great Movie Ride)

Answers to Disney-MGM Studios' Sunset Boulevard

SB-1: Gray with black trim (shop opposite Anaheim Produce); **SB-2:** playing polo, swimming, ice skating, or playing tennis (photos on wall at Mouse About Town shop); **SB-3:** A mosquito—it's a prop from Jurassic Park (on wall in Planet Hollywood shop); **SB-5:** Once Upon a Time character sketches (on marquee above shop entrance); **SB-6:** Theater of the Stars (sign at theatre, may also appear on guidemaps); **SB-8:** Red (outside building for Rock 'n' Roller Coaster); **SB-9:** Paris Luxury Cosmetiques (corner opposite shop exit—the shop is at the exit to Tower of Terror); **SB-10:** 1917 (sign at entrance to the ride building); **SB-11:** 25 cents (noted at box office for Legends of Hollywood); **SB-12:** 414 to 426 (seen while riding Tower of Terror); **SB-13:** 694 (corner of Sunset and Highlands); **SB-14:** 1928 (plaque beside entrance on building); **SB-16:** Anaheim Produce (Sunset Ranch Market); **SB-17:** (sign is to the left of the large guitar, and is both the ride exit and the entrance for those who wish to just shop); **SB-15:** 77 Sunset (corner of Sunset and Gower); **SB-19:** California (display rack to right as you exit ride); **SB-20:** Desert Hot Springs Ice Company (second floor window by restrooms on side street); **SB-21:** E = MC² (seen while riding Tower of Terror); **SB-23:** Beverly, Fountain, and Sunset (just before the Tower Gallery shop); **SB-23:** G-Force Records (seen on various items in Rock 'n' Roller Coaster queue); **SB-24:** Golden Arches Farms (printed on potato sacks At the exclusive Tower Gallery (second entrance to the right on the outside of the building as you exit the gift shop); **SB-22:** Evil Tower U R Doomed (directory in lobby of Hollywood Tower Hotel); **SB-26:** Kelloggs (billboard on top of building); **SB-28:** Victory and signs at the french fry stand); **SB-25:** Harbor your Hunger (sign above the building in the food service area of Sunset Boulevard); **SB-27:** OKLIMO, UGOGIRL, BUHBYE, 2FAST4U, and H8TRFFC (seen while boarding Rock 'n' Roller Coaster); **SB-28:** Victory with Vegetables (Next to Catalina in the Sunset Ranch Market food service area); **SB-29:** The Scaredy Cats (on wall in queue of Rock 'n' Roller Coaster); **SB-30:** The superstretch limo (on Rock 'n' Roller Coaster entrance); **SB-32:** 8:05 (appears as you see the glamourous couple walking through the lobby); **SB-33:** Exxon (billboard above Villians in Vogue store); **SB-34:** Five employees disappeared at The Hollywood Tower Hotel on Halloween 1939 (on wall in queue of Rock 'n' Roller Coaster); **SB-35:** July 29, 1999 (signed picture at the exit of Rock N' Roller Coaster); **SB-36:** Peach Shortcake, Apple Pie and Cream, Gâteau Chocolate au Rotman (menu can be found on the wall to the right of the photo pickup registers, just before you enter the gift shop); **SB-37:** Solve the Case, Save the Dame and Get the Dame (movie poster at entrance to the Planet Hollywood Super Store); **SB-38:** R.T. (Tower of Terror queue); **SB-39:** Sound Horn (Behind Planet Hollywood near the restrooms); **SB-40:** Stunt Dogs (second floor window above Sunset Club Couture); **SB-41:** The Gamewell Company (phone is located on Highland near the side entrance to the Once Upon a Time shop); **SB-42:** Wicked Queen/Dragon in windows, from Snow White; and Maleficent/Hag over candy displays, from Sleeping Beauty (candy shop in the Sunset Ranch Market food service area); **SB-43:** Rosie's All American Cafe (sign in the Sunset Ranch Market food service area)

Answers to Disney-MGM Studios' Echo Lake

EL-1: Holly Vermont (sign next to the Frozen Coke stand); **EL-2:** Coca-Cola (on roof of Hollywood and Vine restaurant); **EL-3:** Third Annual (on plaque at statue display by Sounds Dangerous); **EL-4:** S.S. Down the Hatch (painted on sign of boat on Echo Lake); **EL-5:** Green (shop near exit of Indiana Jones Show); **EL-6:** Unda Cova (billboard for Sounds Dangerous); **EL-7:** Nickels (printed on phone in booth on back left side of Backlot Express); **EL-8:** Stage 12 (sign by entrance on left side); **EL-9:** above Keystone Clothiers (across from Min & Bill's Dockside Diner); **EL-10:** 1914 (sign at Gertie the Dinosaur on Echo Lake); **EL-11:** 428 (sign on the door of 50s Prime Time Cafe); **EL-12:** 4:00 (desk next to the stroller parking sign near Indiana Jones entrance); **EL-13:** 5380 (sign inside the Star Tours building entrance); **EL-14:** 75 cents (sign in second story window above Indiana Jones show entrance); **EL-15:** A fuel truck (seen during Star Tours); **EL-16:** Tatooine (heard during Star Tours); **EL-17:** Denman Island (back corner of Backlot Express); **EL-18:** G2-9T (Audio-Animatronics robot seen just before entrance to Star Tours boarding area); **EL-19:** Lucille Ball (statue display by Sounds Dangerous); **EL-20:** Min and Bill (sign outside the Dockside Diner); **EL-21:** Money, Save It (blue sign on the ramp at Backlot Express); **EL-22:** Paper bag (heard during Sounds Dangerous); **EL-23:** Pull (Or Don't Pull depending on how exactly you read the sign) (sign near well in front of Indiana Jones show); **EL-24:** Punching another employee's card (a time clock located to the left of the counter area); **EL-25:** Red and White (seen during Indiana Jones show); **EL-26:** Remove before flight (tag is on Captain Rex); **EL-27:** Sector 2 (overhead announcements and several signs in Star Tours queue); **EL-28:** Slasher (heard during Sounds Dangerous); **EL-29:** Waterloo, Iowa (back wall near the Paint Office at Backlot Express); **EL-30:** The Great Rinaldi (heard during Sounds Dangerous); **EL-31:** Three (seen during Indiana Jones show); **EL-32:** Three (seen during Star Tours pre-boarding film);

EL-33: Undercover Live (heard during Sounds Dangerous); **EL-34:** 1928 (above the entrance to Hollywood & Vine); **EL-35:** 1119 (announced as your shuttle is turning the wrong way for departure on Star Tours); **EL-37:** VM2465 (back of Jeep seen in last scene of Indiana Jones show); **EL-36:** ST-45 (announced at various times during Star Tours entrance queue); **EL-38:** T-20.4 (announced as you are about to leave the Star Tours facility); **EL-39:** Thursday, December 15, 1988 (bulletin board of paint shop in Backlot Express); **EL-40:** Jonesboro County (crate outside Min and Bill's Dockside Diner); **EL-41:** Elephant (heard during Sounds Dangerous); **EL-42:** T. Kirk (mailboxes by the stairway between 50s Prime Time Cafe and Hollywood & Vine); **EL-43:** 540 Echo Park Drive, #204 (next to the frozen Coke stand); **EL-44:** 2905 Burton Drive, Canbra CA 93428 (Paint Department bulletin board in Backlot Express); **EL-45:** Eighteen (seen during Indiana Jones show); **EL-46:** Temple of the Forbidden Eye Excavation Office, Lost Delta, India (shipping crate near the Dip Site near Indiana Jones show);

Answers to Disney-MGM Studios' Streets of America — **SA-1:** A flying saucer (sign on side of Sci-Fi Dine-In Theater); **SA-2:** A torch and a heart-shaped box of chocolates (fountain in front of Muppet*Vision 3-D entrance); **SA-3:** Making a lasso (next to billboard on Toy Story Pizza Planet); **SA-4:** Orange (on various signs for Toy Story Pizza Planet); **SA-5:** 11 (ceiling of Toy Story Pizza Planet); **SA-6:** The moon (Al's Toy Barn is behind Mama Melrose's Ristorante Italiano); **SA-7:** A cow udder (next to mural at Al's Toy Barn); **SA-8:** (big sign at entrance to Lights, Motors, Action!); **SA-9:** 25 mph (posted sign on New York Street); **SA-10:** 20 West 40th Street (directory at the building on the New York Street in Streets of America); **SA-11:** Teung Ho (on the alleyway halfway down the street); **SA-12:** David L. Davies (Gillespie Street intersects with New York Street in Streets of America); **SA-13:** $235 (posted sign on New York Street); **SA-14:** A bicycle (Brockerhoff on New York Street); **SA-15:** A flower pot (seen in pre-show film of Muppet*Vision 3-D); **SA-16:** A prettier place to be (door in the entrance area of Muppet*Vision 3-D); **SA-17:** Gold and diamonds (sign in the window on New York Street); **SA-18:** "For the halibut" (heard at the beginning of Muppet*Vision 3-D); **SA-19:** Get out of here fast (sign in the Muppet Store near the exit of Muppet*Vision 3-D); **SA-20:** Kermit (movie marker board in pre-show area of Muppet*Vision 3-D); **SA-21:** Max (heard in pre-show film of Muppet*Vision 3-D); **SA-22:** Mickey Mouse (seen in pre-show film of Muppet*Vision 3-D); **SA-23:** More sugar (heard during Muppet*Vision 3-D); **SA-24:** Sets off the fireworks (Gonzo—he asks for his payment from Gonzo after Sam the Eagle kicks him out); **SA-25:** Ten bucks (heard during Muppet*Vision 3-D); **SA-26:** The key (look under the mat under the box office window on the right side the entrance to Muppet*Vision 3-D); **SA-27:** The Muppet Labs Dept. of Wild Guesses (wait time sign at the entrance to Muppet*Vision 3-D, and sometimes in the daily parade); **SA-28:** The Swedish Chef (seen during Muppet*Vision 3-D); **SA-29:** Three (pre-show area of Muppet*Vision 3-D); **SA-30:** Three (seen during Muppet*Vision 3-D); **SA-31:** YO (mural on the back wall of the Toy Story Pizza Planet); **SA-32:** Kermit the Frog (mural at the front of the Muppet*Vision 3-D pre-show); **SA-33:** Newark, NJ (box at the front of the Muppet*Vision 3-D pre-show area); **SA-34:** A football team (heard during Muppet*Vision 3-D); **SA-35:** $9.99 (Sal's pawn shop is located halfway down New York Street on the right hand side if you enter from Star Tours); **SA-36:** A Magic Shop (look above Mama Melrose's Ristorante Italiano); **SA-37:** green (pre-show area of Muppet*Vision 3D); **SA-38:** Muppet*Vision 3D); **SA-39:** The Committee to Keep Miss Piggy Happy (Miss Piggy billboard on top of building across from Al's Toy Barn); **SA-40:** On wall behind hotel desk (at rear of Muppet Shop Stage One Company Store)

Answers to Disney-MGM Studios' Mickey Avenue — **MA-1:** Three (sign over entrance to playground); **MA-2:** Studio Catering Co. (near "Honey, I Shrunk the Kids" playground); **MA-3:** Suspended from ceiling (near "Splash" (in front of Studios Backlot Tour); **MA-4:** Madison Street (in front of the building); **MA-5:** M. Mouse (sign on the outside of the Mickey Mouse greeting area); **MA-6:** Under the rock ledge Ariel is sitting on (above Voyage of the Little Mermaid); **MA-7:** Sorcerer's hat (sign above The Magic of Disney Animation); **MA-8:** 5 (large sign on the side of the Playhouse Disney building); **MA-9:** A space rocket (large sign on top of Playhouse Disney building); **MA-10:** Dr. Tom's (in display case in wooden floor area of One Man's Dream); **MA-11:** 14 stories (plaque beside display case across from One Man's Dream theater); **MA-12:** 8 oz. (printed on "bottle" on Mickey Avenue); **MA-13:** 1906 (on wall of wooden floor area in One Man's Dream); **MA-14:** Ages 2 and up (Play-Doh canister in "Honey, I Shrunk the Kids' playground); **MA-15:** 1964–65 New York World's Fair (on wall in 1960s area across from the WED Studios Epcot display in One Man's Dream); **MA-16:** C-41 (painted on side of film roll in playground); **MA-17:** Ariel (seen during Voyage of the Little Mermaid); **MA-18:** Flounder (Flounder does several flips after the blowfish blows at him during his starring moment in the song "Under the Sea" in Voyage of the Little Mermaid); **MA-19:** Four swans (under Dumbo model in 1950s area of One Man's Dream); **MA-20:** L.J. Silver (sign near the animator's drawing desk in wooden floor area of One Man's Dream); **MA-21:** He "sniffs" you! (giant Quark in "Honey, I Shrunk the Kids' playground); **MA-22:** Green, pink, blue, and orange (seen during Voyage of the Little Mermaid); **MA-23:** Luna (seen and heard during Playhouse Disney); **MA-24:** M.J. Winkler (sign near the animator's desk in wooden floor area of the Mickey Ave. sign near Studios Backlot Tour entrance); **MA-25:** Red (seen in playground); **MA-26:** Reluctant Dragon (sign on the wall during One Man's Dream); **MA-27:** Sixteen (heard during Voyage of the Little Mermaid); **MA-28:** Three (seen during Voyage of the Little Mermaid); **MA-29:** Six (heard during One Man's Dream film); **MA-30:** The World's Fair building (heard during One Man's Dream); **MA-31:** Tinkerbell's (pre-show area of Voyage of the Little Mermaid); **MA-32:** The Tiny Voice (next to the model of Main Street, U.S.A in One Man's Dream); **MA-33:** The Old Colony Theater (seen during One Man's Dream film); **MA-34:** Inside Monstro (On the wall, just before the entrance to the theater at Voyage of the Little Mermaid); **MA-35:** The Los Angeles Times; **MA-36:** Chicago (heard during One Man's Dream film); **MA-37:** 1931 (heard during One Man's Dream film); **MA-38:** The Los Angeles Times (across from Granny's Cabin model in One Man's Dream); **MA-39:** Mae West (letter in the Silly Symphony display near the animator's desk in the 1965 Audio-Animatronics studio of One Man's Dream); **MA-40:** Cardboard (heard during One Man's Dream); **MA-41:** 5 Million Dollars (heard during One Man's Dream)

Answers to Photos Under the Treasure Chest — **MGM-A:** Outdoor seating area in Backlot Express; **MGM-B:** Hanging from clock atop Muppet*Vision 3D; **MGM-C:** On door near frozen Coke stand across from Hollywood & Vine; **MGM-D:** On San Francisco Mural (Streets of America); **MGM-E:** In statue garden across from Echo Lake

Under the Treasure Chest

Where in Disney-MGM Studios
can you find these five images?

(Answers are inside the treasure chest,
of course!)

MGM-A

MGM-B

MGM-C

MGM-D

MGM-E

Treasure Chest #4
Disney's Animal Kingdom

Open chest (tear perforation) to view the Animal Kingdom answers.

Answers to Disney's Animal Kingdom's Oasis and Discovery Island

DI-1: Rainforest Cafe (on left as you approach the park entrance); **DI-2:** Kodak (sign on store, which is located on right after park entrance); **DI-3:** Rhinoceros Iguanas (sign on right entrance path near hyacinth macaws); **DI-4:** Bird (bridge between The Oasis and Discovery Island); **DI-5:** Beaver (near bridge that leads back to the trail to Camp Minnie-Mickey); **DI-6:** Kangaroo (just before the trail to Discovery Island); **DI-7:** Butterflies (west side of Discovery Island); **DI-8:** Ladybugs (just north of Pizzafari); **DI-9:** Whistle (sign in The Tree of Life garden near Island Mercantile); **DI-10:** Near drinking fountains (sign right after you cross the bridge into Discovery Island); **DI-11:** Disappearing wetlands (sign on the path between left and right entrance walks in The Oasis); **DI-12:** Buzzing, stinging, pollenating, or chirping (this announcement is made just as lights go down at the start of the "It's Tough to Be a Bug!" show); **DI-13:** A turtle (just before the bridge that leads into Asia); **DI-14:** An acorn weevil (sign just before you enter the theater's waiting area in "It's Tough to Be a Bug!" queue); **DI-15:** Hyacinth Macaw (sign on the left side of the right/east path in The Oasis, just before the stone archway); **DI-16:** 35,000 (The Webside Story theater poster in the indoor waiting area for "It's Tough to Be a Bug!" show); **DI-17:** Pig-Deer (sign on right/east entrance path at the stone archway in The Oasis); **DI-18:** 30,000 bugs per day (sign on left/west path in The Oasis); **DI-19:** "Hi Mom!" (theater poster in indoor waiting area for "It's Tough to Be a Bug!" show); **DI-20:** African Spoonbill (The Oasis near park entrance); **DI-21:** Bug Doom (the audience is sprayed with Bug Doom as Hopper gives his presentation); **DI-22:** Collared and Ring-Tailed Lemurs (behind FASTPASS distribution area for "It's Tough to Be a Bug!" show); **DI-23:** Wild (Rainforest Cafe signs); **DI-24:** Fireflies (Flik directs the fireflies to shine on him at the beginning of the "It's Tough to Be a Bug!" show); **DI-25:** A Bug's Life (as far as we're aware, this is the only place you can find Princess Atta in the parks); **DI-26:** "Hello, Dung Lovers" (theater poster in indoor waiting area for "It's Tough to Be a Bug!" show); **DI-27:** Gorilla (Creature Comforts shop, just before the bridge that leads to Africa); **DI-28:** A dynamic "boo doo" duo (sign just before you enter the theater's waiting area in "It's Tough to Be a Bug!" queue); **DI-29:** A fish (southeast corner of Discovery Island, near entrance to DinoLand U.S.A.); **DI-30:** At least 60,000 flowers (theater poster in indoor waiting area for "It's Tough to Be a Bug!" show); **DI-31:** 55 boards (it looks like a lot less, until you start counting); **DI-32:** Camels (Island Mercantile, to the left as you enter Discovery Island from The Oasis); **DI-33:** Tree of Life Repertory Theatre (theater poster in the indoor waiting area for "It's Tough to Be a Bug!" queue); **DI-34:** Chameleons (Pizzafari, near path leading to Camp Minnie-Mickey); **DI-35:** Tim Burr (The Termite-ator sign just before you enter the theater waiting area in "It's Tough to Be a Bug!" show); **DI-36:** Axis Deer (sign in The Tree of Life garden, near Island Mercantile shop); **DI-37:** Helps take care of the young chicks after they hatch (sign on path between left and right entrance walks in The Oasis); **DI-38:** 3,000 ladybugs (The My Fair Ladybug theater poster in indoor waiting area for "It's Tough to Be a Bug!" show); **DI-39:** The yellow spot adorning its bill (sign on path between left and right entrance walks in The Oasis); **DI-40:** Soft clay (sign next to the Safari Popcorn and "It's Tough to Be a Bug!" entrance); **DI-41:** "A real stinker" according to the Odorlando Scenti-nal (theater poster in indoor waiting area for "It's Tough to Be a Bug!" show); **DI-42:** Cygnus atratus (sign in pond area just inside the turnstiles, near Garden Gate Gifts); **DI-43:** Blue (sign on path between left and right entrance walks in The Oasis); **DI-44:** Up to 600 pounds according to the Tree of Life Garden—make a left as you exit "It's Tough to Be a Bug!" to find this hidden area)

Answers to Disney's Animal Kingdom's Camp Minnie-Mickey

MM-1: Bridge to Camp Minnie-Mickey; **MM-2:** Four (shown on guidemaps); **MM-3:** Pocahontas and The Lion King (signs, guidemaps); **MM-4:** Adirondacks in New York (noted on guidemaps, signs); **MM-5:** Blue/gray (beside brook on right as you cross bridge toward Festival of the Lion King); **MM-6:** Two (signs, guidemaps); **MM-7:** A boot (submerged in brook on right as you cross bridge toward Festival of the Lion King); **MM-8:** Hexagon (you can see the shape on guidemaps and also when you're inside the theater); **MM-9:** In the Camp Minnie-Mickey area (guidemaps, signs); the seating area sections are named by the performers at the start of the show); **MM-10:** Four: elephant, giraffe, warthog, and lion (the seating area sections are named by the performers at the start of the show); **MM-11:** Simba, Pumbaa, and Timon (Simba and Pumbaa are on floats, Timon walks around during the show); **MM-12:** Daisy (on right along stream bank as you enter Camp Minnie-Mickey); **MM-13:** Elephant (Festival of the Lion King); **MM-14:** Grandmother Willow (introduced during show); **MM-15:** To character greetings with Pooh and friends (signs in Camp Minnie-Mickey); **MM-16:** Entrances are in the shape of Mickey (throughout Camp Minnie-Mickey); **MM-17:** Acrobats in monkey costumes (Festival of the Lion King); **MM-18:** On your right as you cross bridge into Camp Minnie-Mickey (it's a small waterfall); **MM-19:** Grandmother Willow (in Pochantas and Her Forest Friends, and in Sounds of the Rainforest at Rafiki's Planet Watch)

Answers to Disney's Animal Kingdom's Africa and Rafiki's PlanetWatch

AF-1: Harambe (various signs around Africa); **AF-2:** 1420 (sign on main walkway in Africa, across from Tusker House); **AF-3:** take a shower (sign on showers near Dawa Bar); **AF-4:** Good Food (hanging sign on Tusker House); **AF-5:** Duka La Filimu (on left before the public laundry room outside Mombasa Marketplace); **AF-6:** Harambe Orientation Centre (various signs around Africa); **AF-7:** 1st Thursday Monthly, Enquire for Times (Tusker House Harambe Orientation Centre dining room); **AF-8:** 1992 (sign at the door of Mombasa Marketplace); **AF-9:** Budget camping (various signs around Harambe); **AF-10:** Eastern Star Railway (painted on train); **AF-11:** Tusker House (model ship on shelf in dining area); **AF-12:** Ten (on beach behind Tusker House); **AF-13:** A boat (on beach behind Tusker House); **AF-14:** Two clipboards (Okapi area at Pangani Trail); **AF-15:** R. Ongala (drum area to the right of entrance to Africa); **AF-16:** Crocodile and Hippo (signs just after aviary at Pangani Trail); **AF-17:** "Following response" (Pangani Forest Exploration Trail); **AF-18:** Wander (sign at Dawa Bar beside Tusker House); **AF-19:** Two hippos (hippo exhibit at Pangani Trail); **AF-20:** Four (mole rat exhibit at Pangani Trail); **AF-21:** 2000 years old (mentioned during Kilimanjaro Safaris ride); **AF-22:** Grass (sign in Pangani Trail); **AF-23:** The giraffe (mentioned during Kilimanjaro Safaris and on sign along Pangani Trail); **AF-24:** Sable antelope (on signs at Kilimanjaro Safaris); **AF-25:** Bongo (mentioned during Kilimanjaro Safaris ride); **AF-26:** "On Holiday" (assignment board on wall in Tusker House); **AF-27:** Social evil (on sign at Rafiki's Planet Watch train station (Africa side)); **AF-28:** Petroleum tank (back of trucks ridden in during Kilimanjaro Safaris—they are visible while waiting in the queue); **AF-29:** No. 4 (map at start of Pangani Trail); **AF-30:** Wild animals always have the right of way (Kilimanjaro Safaris queue bridge); **AF-31:** Naples, Florida (sign at Conservation Station in Rafiki's Planet Watch); **AF-32:** Mia Fari (sign on pole outside Mombasa Marketplace); **AF-33:** Dawkins (Pangani Forest Exploration Trail); **AF-34:** Debra Murunga (exit of Pangani Trail); **AF-35:** Dawkins (Pangani Forest Exploration Trail); **AF-36:** They will become a disturbance (sign on the back patio of Tusker House); **AF-37:** Cheetah (signs in Kilimanjaro Safaris queue); **AF-38:** PhD (queue video for Kilimanjaro Safaris ride); **AF-39:** 100 (sign at the Ziwani Traders store); **AF-40:** Purple (seen during latter half of Kilimanjaro Safaris ride); **AF-41:** S1775 (on window outside of

Tusker House across from Mombasa Marketplace); **AF-42:** The station master (by the luggage area of the Africa train station); **AF-43:** Warden Post #6 (gorilla area at Pangani Trail); **AF-44:** PO Box 187, Telephone: 53609 (sign at the Ziwani Traders store); **AF-45:** East Africa Railroad (seen right before the red clay pits about 3/4 through Kilimanjaro Safaris); **AF-46:** Carlos (sign as the tamarind exhibit at Affection Section petting zoo at Rafiki's Planet Watch); **AF-47:** The road (sign in front of the accessible load area of Kilimanjaro Safaris); **AF-48:** Cooking forbidden (written in Eastern Star Railway car that travels to/from Tusker House and at the Dawa Bar); **AF-49:** Dangerous Currents (sign behind Tusker House and at the Dawa Bar); **AF-50:** Anything it can (noted on clipboard to the left of the Research Center entrance on Pangani Forest Exploration Trail)

Answers to Disney's Animal Kingdom's Asia — **AS-1:** Four spires (on four corners of bridge); **AS-2:** Elephant (sign on path to Anandapur); **AS-3:** Caravan Stage (sign on wall on main path, right of exit); **AS-4:** Dragons (in dining area of Chakranadi Chicken Shop); **AS-5:** Royal (printed on quidemap and signs in area); **AS-6:** White Water (sign at Kali River Rapids FASTPASS kiosk); **AS-7:** Two (exit bridge at end of Kali River Rapids); **AS-8:** Chakranadi River (printed on quidemap and signs in area); **AS-9:** Next Season (sign on first building on Expedition Everest from Anandapur); **AS-10:** The fire fell off (on path as you walk into Asia); **AS-11:** On the big tree (as you enter Asia); **AS-12:** 1948 (sign outside Maharajah Jungle Trek); **AS-13:** 4.0 Kilograms (sign on tank outside Gupta's); **AS-14:** A raft (look for the painting of rafts with interesting names as you are about to cross the bridge to board Kali River Rapids); **AS-15:** An Internet Cafe (sign on the second story of the restroom building); **AS-16:** Anandapur Travel and Tourism (sign near Mandala gift shop); **AS-17:** Anandapur Telegraphy (sign near restrooms between Asia and DinoLand U.S.A.); **AS-18:** Annapurna (inside Drinkwallah); **AS-19:** Bells (Kali River Rapids queue); **AS-20:** Bugis Sea (map in Kali River Rapids queue); **AS-21:** Chakranadi River (sign outside of Maharajah Jungle Trek); **AS-22:** Five persons (sign on fountains); **AS-23:** Kali River Expedition (start of queue for Kali River Rapids); **AS-24:** U.S. dollars (sign on the shop's safe in the Kali River Rapids queue); **AS-25:** Two statues (Kali River Rapids queue); **AS-26:** Mr. Panika (Kali River Rapids queue); **AS-27:** No. 0015 (on the walkway that passes by Expedition Everest); **AS-28:** Saturday (calendar is outside the bat viewing area, between the two doors, in Maharajah Jungle Trek); **AS-29:** Shoes (signs at Kali River Rapids); **AS-30:** Sunaulo Toran (quidemaps and signs); **AS-31:** Swooping and soaring (sign outside the theater); **AS-32:** The Anandapur Rural Electrification Programme (sign on poles near exit of Kali River Rapids); **AS-33:** Three pitchers (Maharajah Jungle Trek); **AS-34:** Three small islands in Indonesia (Komodo Dragon sign on Maharajah Jungle Trek); **AS-35:** Friday (sign in the bat house on Maharajah Jungle Trek); **AS-36:** Six statues (seen while riding Kali River Rapids); **AS-37:** Flying Yak (bottom right of the sign just to the right of Mandala Gifts); **AS-38:** 6993 (picture of mountain range in Drinkwallah); **AS-39:** 600 insects (sign in bat house on Maharajah Jungle Trek— the sign is located between the two doors and opposite the bat viewing area); **AS-40:** Tetak Logging (seen while riding Kali River Rapids); **AS-41:** Bhavani Sign Painting (sign at the restrooms between DinoLand U.S.A. and Asia, near the Everest side of the building); **AS-42:** 225615 (sign to the left side of Mandala Gifts listing phone numbers for Anandapur); **AS-43:** Fans (sign in Kali River Rapids queue); **AS-44:** Maraslu Slammer (raft status board if boarding Kali River Rafts); **AS-45:** Eight stories (second set of four is around the very top of the building); **AS-46:** Tigers (sign just past bat house on the right side of the path); **AS-47:** Manesha Gurung (lifeguard qualification plaque in Kali River Rapids queue); **AS-48:** Bob (picture inside Drinkwallah, opposite the counter)

Answers to Disney's Animal Kingdom's DinoLand U.S.A. — **DL-1:** Oldengate Bridge (sign on left of bridge as you enter the land, under rear right foot); **DL-2:** 25 mph (signs on the roadway outside of Chester & Hester's Dino-Rama); **DL-3:** Four persons (visible by watching the Primeval Whirl vehicles from the ground); **DL-4:** Diggs County (numerous signs throughout DinoLand U.S.A.); **DL-5:** An engine (auto repair room); **DL-6:** Seebug (Hip Joint room); **DL-7:** 1947 ("bone" sign over entrance to The Boneyard); **DL-8:** Three chutes (visible by walking around the Boneyard); **DL-9:** Jenny Weinstein (on top of the T-Rex hill); **DL-10:** Dino Sue, the replica Tyrannosaurus Rex (near the entrance to Dinosaur); **DL-11:** 10,000 years ago (sign on bridge); **DL-12:** Jenny W. (fossil matrix sign in The Boneyard); **DL-13:** 96 (Hip Joint seating area of Restaurantosaurus); **DL-14:** Gold (seen in Dinosaur pre-show video); **DL-15:** Prerrace (sign at Restaurantosaurus); **DL-16:** A. Canthus (near register area at Restaurantosaurus); **DL-17:** 30 feet or 9 meters (display in The Boneyard); **DL-18:** Ice Age (sign seen while riding Primeval Whirl); **DL-19:** 611 (Chester & Hester's Dinosaur Treasures store); **DL-20:** "In the past" (heard in Dinosaur pre-show video); **DL-21:** Stegosoa (Hip Joint seating area of Restaurantosaurus) and in the very first part of the ride as you go back in time); **DL-22:** Green (located in the loading area of Dinosaur and in the very first part of the ride as you go back in time); **DL-23:** 7:00 am (chalkboard display in the Boneyard); **DL-24:** 2:55 PM (back of Primeval Whirl vehicles); **DL-25:** 21 sites (map at DVC kiosk near Dino-Bite Snacks/Restaurantosaurus); **DL-26:** Four scientists (Primeval Whirl queue area); **DL-27:** Squirt water (water gun display in the seating area immediately to the right of the counter); **DL-28:** Number 3 (edge of Cretaceous Trail near Chester & Hester's); **DL-29:** 5 seconds (signs at end of Primeval Whirl); **DL-30:** 5 seconds (signs at end of Primeval Whirl); **DL-31:** Dr. B. Dunn (sign at the entrance to The Boneyard); **DL-32:** $2 (sign behind Chester & Hester's store and Primeval Whirl); **DL-33:** A cat (roof above entrance to Restaurantosaurus); **DL-34:** Yellow (seen while riding Primeval Whirl); **DL-35:** Pedestrian (pedestrian crossing sign by theater in the Wild); **DL-36:** Carnotaurus (it's written on the side of the fossil display case at Restaurantosaurus); **DL-37:** 1960 (Hip Joint seating area of Restaurantosaurus); **DL-38:** 41 cents per gallon (Chester & Hester's); **DL-39:** The Brachiosaurus (signs outside The Boneyard); **DL-40:** Older than dirt (load area and lift hill of Primeval Whirl); **DL-41:** Grosvenor House (Disney Vacation Club kiosk); **DL-42:** The Road (entrance to the Vehicle Maintenance area of Restaurantosaurus); **DL-43:** 32 cents (counter area of Restaurantosaurus); **DL-44:** Their heads (sign in The Boneyard); **DL-45:** Can Opener (fossil room display case at Restaurantosaurus); **DL-46:** 555-1987 (note on the wall next to the payphone in Chester & Hester's); **DL-47:** May 24th (sign in the loft above the right hand seating area of Restaurantosaurus)

Answers to Photos Under the Treasure Chest — **AK-A:** Well near stream in Camp Minnie-Mickey (Discovery Island); **AK-B:** Framed plaque in west dining room at Tusker House (Africa); **AK-C:** Statue outside of Pizzafari near path to Camp Minnie-Mickey (Discovery Island); **AK-D:** Petrifies sign on your right as you enter DinoLand); **AK-E:** Top of pole in Gibbon habitat (Asia)

Under the Treasure Chest

Where in Disney's Animal Kingdom can you find these five images?

(Answers are inside the treasure chest, of course!)

AK-A

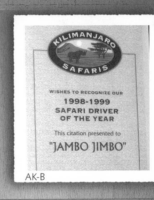

AK-B

AK-C

AK-D

MK-E

Treasure Chest #5
Downtown Disney

Open chest (tear perforation) to view the Downtown Disney answers.

Answers to Downtown Disney's Marketplace

MP-1: Leaping (along the mural outside the Disney's of Days Christmas); **MP-2:** Behind the personalization counter (Disney's Days of Christmas); **MP-3:** Rabbit (Team Disney store); **MP-4:** Tinkertoys (between Earl of Sandwhich and Once Upon a Toy); **MP-5:** Woody (Once Upon a Toy store); **MP-6:** Cinderella Castle (Disney Bear room at Once Upon a Toy); **MP-7:** Tinkerbell (top of exterior of World of Disney); **MP-8:** Mickey's hands (fitting rooms inside World of Disney); **MP-9:** Hearts (Alice room at World of Disney); **MP-10:** "Ski Mars" (in front of Lego Store); **MP-11:** On top of the World of Disney store (being held by Tweedle Dum, or is it Dee?); **MP-12:** 60 minutes (in front of Lego Store); **MP-13:** 1817–1894 (Outside wall of Ghiradelli's Shop); **MP-14:** Hunchback display by Wonderful World of Memories (Disney's Days of Christmas); **MP-15:** July 1, 2004 (behind the register in Disney Tails shop); **MP-16:** Cheshire Cat (World of Disney); **MP-17:** Daisy Duck (wall art in the hat room at World of Disney); **MP-18:** Bennie the Cab (the mural along the top of the wall in World of Disney); **MP-19:** A soccer ball (Team Mickey sign); **MP-20:** Along the ornament wall (Disney's Days of Christmas); **MP-21:** Tracy Tree (Retail Village shop at Rainforest Café); **MP-22:** Painting (on the fireplace at Disney's Days of Christmas); **MP-23:** An accordian (sign outside Cap'n Jack's Restaurant)

Answers to Downtown Disney's Pleasure Island

PI-1: Swinging her leg (near large neon Pleasure Island display on back of West End Stage building at west end of island); **PI-2:** 1911 (plaque near entrance and ticket booths); **PI-3:** 21 or older (sign near entrance to Mannequins); **PI-4:** A shark with sunglasses (sign above Rock'n'Roll Beach Club); **PI-5:** 17 stars are on the building, not counting any on windows or doors (Reel Finds is behind Mannequins); **PI-6:** Maxwell's Alley (street sign in front of 8Trax); **PI-7:** A parachute (top of Adventurers Club); **PI-8:** Adventurers Club (on sign on Adventurers Club); **PI-9:** In the Comedy Warehouse logo (sign on Comedy Warehouse); **PI-10:** The Who, What and Warehouse Improv Company (sign on front of Comedy Warehouse); **PI-11:** Comedy Warehouse; **PI-12:** PI (Comedy Warehouse exit); **PI-13:** 1928 (plaque on Comedy Warehouse building); **PI-14:** Merriweather's canvas fabrication works, Invincible Pictures, and a design studio/workshop (plaque outside the entrance to Mannequins); **PI-15:** Isabella (plaque on Portobello Yacht Club); **PI-16:** December 31, 1937 (since it's New Years Eve every night on Pleasure Island and it's 1937 in the Adventurers Club according to its entrance sign, it's always December 31, 1937); **PI-17:** 21.1 cents (near the stairs to West Side); **PI-18:** Stem to Stern, we've got you covered (sign on side of West End Stage over the restrooms); **PI-19:** Since 1918 (sign on the back side of West End Stage near the water); **PI-20:** 1933 during a party celebrating the repeal of Prohibition (plaque on The Island Depot building); **PI-21:** Pleasure Perfect Upholstery (sign under Yakoose head in Main Salon of Adventurers Club, and plaque on Changing Attitudes shop); **PI-22:** Adam (plaque near entrance and ticket booths, and on Suspended Animation building); **PI-23:** Four people (Library inside the Adventurers Club); **PI-24:** Grapes (Mask Room of Adventurers Club)

Answers to Downtown Disney's West Side

WS-1: Jenny, the shrimping vessel from "Forrest Gump" (in water on left side of Planet Hollywood); **WS-2:** Blue (beside AMC Theaters); **WS-3:** Red (sign on upper corner of Starabilias shop); **WS-4:** Caramel apple (sign above Candy Cauldron shop); **WS-5:** far right side of back wall (inside Candy Cauldron shop); **WS-6:** Live, Love, Eat (sign above Wolfgang Puck's); **WS-7:** A Mickey head (DisneyQuest signs); **WS-8:** Planet Hollywood (store across from center plaza); **WS-9:** Silver (beside Bongo's); **WS-10:** Two signs (water tower beside House of Blues); **WS-11:** A white circus tent, or "Big Top"; **WS-12:** Blues (painted above House of Blues entrance); **WS-13:** Don't steal (sign on wall near the register at House of Blues); **WS-14:** Coco Moka Cafe (signs at Virgin Megastore); **WS-15:** Gold (AMC Theatres); **WS-16:** 38 (between Wetzel's Pretzels and Bongo's Cuban Cafe); **WS-17:** Chinese Water Torture (display window poster at Magic Masters); **WS-18:** 616 State St. (on porch at House of Blues); **WS-19:** Three bars; **WS-20:** Carter the Great (display window poster at Magic Masters); **WS-21:** St. Paul, Minnesota (sign on porch at House of Blues); **WS-22:** Magnetron (next to Candy Cauldron); **WS-23:** Sosa Family Cigars (inside the shop); **WS-24:** Cirque du Soleil (on left as you face the box office)

Answers to Photos Under the Treasure Chest

DD-A: Lamps suspended from ceiling in Disney Tails (Marketplace); **DD-B:** On shelf near ceiling in Planet Hollywood store (West Side); **DD-C:** On porch in front of House of Blues (West Side); **DD-D:** Below cash register in Candy Cauldron (West Side); **DD-E:** on back side of West End Stage (Pleasure Island)

Under the Treasure Chest

Where in Downtown Dsney can you find these five images?

(Answers are inside the treasure chest, of course!)

DD-A

DD-B

DD-C

DD-D

DD-E

Treasure Chest #6
Resorts

Open chest (tear perforation) to view the Resorts answers.

Answers to All-Star Resorts — **AR-1:** Six lights (All-Star Music lobby); **AR-2:** Two sailors (Intermission food court at All-Star Music); **AR-3:** Mighty Ducks (food court at All-Star Sports); **AR-4:** Goofy (pool in Home Run Hotel section of All-Star Sports); **AR-5:** 53 (buildings #6 and #7 at All-Star Movies); **AR-6:** fire hydrants (buildings #1 and #3 at All-Star Sports); **AR-7:** back of Sports Goofy shop; **AR-8:** toy Story courtyard; **AR-9:** on top of Rock Inn; **AR-11:** 42nd and Broadway (Broadway area at All-Star Movies); **AR-12:** Five Xs (between buildings #7 and #10 at All-Star Movies); **AR-13:** 118 persons (sign on pool at All-Star Music); **AR-14:** Four books (101 Dalmatians at All-Star Movies); **AR-15:** Guitar (towards back of All-Star Music); **AR-16:** Sorcerer's Apprentice Mickey (between buildings #5 and #8 at All-Star Sports); **AR-17:** 125 (buildings #8 and #9 at All-Star Sports); **AR-18:** Four soldiers (toy Story staircases at All-Star Music); **AR-19:** Saludos Amigos (theme pool at All-Star Music); **AR-20:** Semernoles, Vols, Rebels, and Cavaliers (between buildings #7 and #10 at All-Star Sports); **AR-21:** Disney's All Star Jazz Band (between buildings #2 and #9 at All-Star Music); **AR-22:** 72 basketballs (buildings #2 and #3 at All-Star Sports)

Answers to Animal Kingdom Lodge — **AK-1:** Welcome (sign in check-in queue in lobby); **AK-2:** Arusha Rock and Ogun's (maps; sign in The Mara eatery); **AK-3:** Three giraffes (sign in The Mara eatery); **AK-6:** Uzima Springs, The Watering Hole (near pool); **AK-7:** Six feet tall (Savanna Overlook); **AK-8:** 6:00 am—9:00 pm (sign at fitness center); **AK-9:** Six feet tall (Giraffe Signs; maps); **AK-11:** Diamond Award (Jiko); **AK-12:** Lobi people (lobby); **AK-13:** The Cooking Place (Jiko); **AK-14:** Ghana (sign displayed with Kente fabric in lobby); **AK-15:** The Cooking Place (Jiko); **AK-16:** Under six years (sign at playground); **AK-17:** Eland (Savanna water sign); **AK-18:** 4:30 pm to midnight (sign at Simba's clubhouse); **AK-19:** S859 (printed on phone); **AK-20:** Africa (lobby); **AK-21:** 2901 Osceola Parkway (inspection certificate in elevator); **AK-22:** Yoruba People (Sunset Overlook); **AK-24:** Oka Johnson (Sunset Overlook); **AK-25:** Acacia (Savanna flora sign); **AK-26:** 45 3/5 15 (in a printed article hanging very near the center of the room. This one is very hard to find)

Answers to BoardWalk — **BW-1:** Boardwalk Bakery (window of bakery); **BW-2:** E. Thompson (store sign); **BW-3:** Madam Morgana (across from the Big River Brewery); **BW-4:** Promenade Pier (sign on dock); **BW-5:** Three elephants (count them); **BW-6:** Five windows (count them); **BW-7:** tremendous Spoonellas (sign); **BW-8:** The clown face on the Keister Coaster slide (Luna Park pool area); **BW-9:** 1902 (store sign near BoardWalk Inn); **BW-10:** The horses have fish tails (BoardWalk Inn); **BW-11:** South (sign above resort entrance); **BW-12:** Exercise for Vim, Vigor & Vitality (on door to fitness center); **BW-13:** 5 mph (sign on walkway); **BW-14:** Green (statue on right side of back wall); **BW-15:** Cottages #1214 and #1215 (at far end of courtyard of BoardWalk Inn); **BW-16:** The Seaside Season is backward and extra attractions are needed; (on the wall by the fitness center and elevators); **BW-17:** 10 cents (in front of roller coaster model in display case in seating area of lobby); **BW-18:** Harrisburg (outside the Inn elevators on the second floor); **BW-19:** 10 cents (outside room 331); **BW-20:** Chicago O'Hare International Airport, NY, and the nation's baseball games (sign on hot dog stand)

Answers to Caribbean Beach — **CB-1:** Two people (Customs House); **CB-2:** Green; **CB-3:** Epcot (you can see the top of Spaceship Earth); **CB-4:** Goombay Games (Old Port Royale); **CB-5:** Seven bus stops (resort maps); **CB-6:** Barefoot Bay Boatyard (near Old Port Royale); **CB-8:** 4 feet (theme pool near Old Port Royale); **CB-9:** 100 persons (sign at pool); **CB-10:** two lion heads (count them) (on either side of "fortress" bridge); **CB-11:** Goofy and Mickey (in corners of chalkboards); **CB-13:** Under the age of 12 (sign at kiddie pool behind Old Port Royale Pool); **CB-14:** Three beaches (resort map in Old Port Royale); **CB-15:** A pineapple (near entrance); **CB-16:** Flavors of the Caribbean (The Old Port Royale Entrance (Outside Main Door)); **CB-18:** The pool bar (beside Old Port Royale Pool); **CB-19:** Meyers Dark Rum, Coconut Rum, Pineapple Juice and Nut Mix (Banana Cabana Pool Bar drink menu); **CB-20:** Between 11am and 2pm except Sundays and Holidays (mailbox near the bell services desk); **CB-21:** Great (wishing fountain at Old Port Royale pool bar); **CB-22:** Twelve (on island in center of turnaround in front of Old Port Royale)

Answers to Contemporary — **CO-1:** Frank Stella (Contemporary lobby); **CO-4:** 178 persons (sign at pool); **CO-5:** Recycle (sides of the recycle/garbage bins); **CO-6:** Mickey and Minnie (near the pool); **CO-7:** Weights (third floor); **CO-8:** Electrical Water Pageant (on the shores of Bay Lake at 10:00 pm); **CO-9:** Must be five feet tall (signs at the marina); **CO-10:** 6:00 pm (entrance to the Convention Center); **CO-11:** M. Stokowski (statue at main entrance (bell services area)); **CO-12:** 57 (on the phone display); **CO-13:** 10:00 am to 5:00 pm (Signs at Sammy Duvall at marina); **CO-14:** Spoon and fork (Fourth floor); **CO-15:** Near the playground (south of North Garden Wing); **CO-16:** Wilderness Lodge and Fort Wilderness (The signs at marina); **CO-18:** Mickey's hand (near the entrance to the eating area); **CO-19:** Blue and white goat (approx. fifth to sixth floor, facing the monorail platform); **CO-20:** Since 1851 (wagon at Settlement Trading Post); **CO-21:** Altering course to starboard (inside of pool bar)

Answers to Coronado Springs — **CS-1:** Blue poles (outside lobby); **CS-2:** La Fuente De Las Palomas (The Fountain of the Pigeons); **CS-3:** Pancho (above the store entrance); **CS-4:** 10:00 pm (arcade sign); **CS-5:** 34 steps (The Dig Site theme pool); **CS-6:** Casitas, Cabanas, and Ranchos (resort maps); **CS-7:** Siestas (The Dig Site theme pool area); **CS-8:** The mouth of a huge statue (Explorer's Playground at The Dig Site); **CS-10:** Four a quiet pool is a each of the three building areas and The Lost City of Cibola feature pool at the Dig Site); **CS-11:** An umbrella (lose is perched on top of a balcony railing in the store); **CS-12:** Birds (Dome of Flowers in lobby ceiling of El Centro); **CS-13:** Francisco's (El Centro); **CS-14:** The Dig Site theme pool (pool map); **CS-15:** Boats and bikes (marina signs); **CS-16:** Up to four guests (the "Water Bee" is a paddle boat available for rental at the marina); **CS-18:** Coronado Circle (road signs); **CS-19:** La Fuente De Las Palomas (Explorer's Playground at The Dig Site); **CS-20:** Tijuana (on yacht in lobby of El Centro); **CS-22:** Lion statues (Lion statues of El Centro); **CS-23:** Jaguar (store area; map); **CS-24:** In case of emergency call 911 (pool area sign); **CS-25:** An open book (on wall in quest check-in area of El Centro); **CS-26:** Jumping Beans Arcade sign (El Centro)

Answers to Fort Wilderness — **FW-1:** Yellow, orange, and purple (resort bus stop signs); **FW-3:** Davy Crockett (Settlement Trading Post); **FW-4:** Daniel Boone (Meadow Trading Post); **FW-6:** 1900 (south section of resort); **FW-7:** "Coonskin," or Davy Crockett, hat (store); **FW-8:** Trail's End Buffeteria (near Pioneer Hall); **FW-9:** Creekside Meadow (resort map); **FW-11:** Trail Blaze Corral (sign at the trail ride meetup point); **FW-12:** None (center of resort); **FW-10:** Vegetable (sign on outside of the Meadow Trading Post); **FW-13:** Lawnmower (sign on tree about halfway between Crockett's Tavern and the marina); **FW-14:** Master Mix (a large aluminum sign to the right of the pool); **FW-16:** Quail Trail (loop 1400); **FW-17:** $10,000 in gold coin (small Wanted poster on the outside of Meadow Trading Post area); **FW-18:** Shuffleboard (Meadow Trading Post area); **FW-19:** Dr. Terminus stagecoach (beside screen); **FW-20:** Since 1851 (wagon at Settlement Trading Post)

Answers to Grand Floridian — **GF-1:** Weather varies; **GF-2:** Octagon (between Grand Lobby and Big Pine Key); **GF-3:** Pylons 118–119 (path that leads south from the Grand Lobby); **GF-4:** Winfield Tennis Courts (signs at tennis courts near Grand Floridian Spa); **GF-5:** Pylons 118–119 (path that leads south from the Grand Lobby); **GF-6:** Gold Flag (boat dock); **GF-8:** 6:00 am (pool deck); **GF-9:** Three (lobby); **GF-10:** Monorail (between Grand Floridian and Polynesian); **GF-11:** Acuote; **GF-12:** 147? (on landing of grand staircase); **GF-13:** Ext. 7-2439 (sign on side of marina building); **GF-14:** 33" (on pool deck); **GF-15:** Lake Buena Vista, Florida (written on stern of yacht); **GF-16:** Octagon (between Grand Floridian and Polynesian); **GF-17:** 1890 (Grand Lobby by grand staircase); **GF-18:** Franck's Studio (between Grand Floridian and Polynesian); **GF-19:** Summer Lace and Sandy Cove (Grand Lobby); **GF-20:** 1823 (outside of Citricos on second floor of Grand Lobby); **GF-21:** Circa 1900 (Grand Lobby); **GF-22:** Great Women (Grand Lobby, second floor); **GF-23:** Behind Summerhouse (between Grand Lobby and Big Pine Key)

Answers to Old Key West — **OK-1:** two parrots (Hospitality House); **OK-2:** Blue arcade sign, near Hospitality House; **OK-3:** R.E.S.T. Beach Recreation Department (Turtle Krawl area near Hospitality House); **OK-4:** White and red; **OK-5:** A giant sandcastle (near Hospitality House); **OK-6:** Disney Vacation Club members; **OK-7:** A yellow sun with Mickey ears (entrance to resort); **OK-8:** A bar (Turtle Krawl area at the Hospitality House); **OK-9:** No bus stops signs (throughout the resort); **OK-10:** Pappa's Den (just off the check-in area at the Hospitality House); **OK-11:** Governor Cobb (on the wall at Olivia's); **OK-12:** PRO BONO PERSONA VENI VIDI VENI AD INFINITUM CARPE DIEM OMNI DIEM (Conch Flats Community Hall); **OK-13:** Hank's (sign at shuffleboard court); **OK-14:** 34 persons (sign at dock); **OK-15:** 1921 (above the shelves in the deli area); **OK-16:** 1510 N Cove Road, Old Key West, Lake Buena Vista, FL 32830 (sign on the wall in the Electric Eel area); **OK-17:** A: Grandy's (on model train in the resort check-in area); **OK-18:** The Laundry (across from R.E.S.T.); **OK-19:** Remington Stands (on the desk in Papa's [be of the check-in area)

Answers to Pop Century — **PC-1:** Diamond (in the 50s section); **PC-2:** Unicycle (on the wall in the 80s/90s section); **PC-3:** A1 Solvents Turpentine (in the 80s/90s section); **PC-4:** 10 function keys (in the 80s/90s sections); **PC-5:** Blue elephant with pink polka dots (in the 60s section); **PC-6:** Duncan (stairwells of the 60s buildings); **PC-7:** Annie Hall (sign on Memory Lane— Annie Hall defeated Star Wars!); **PC-8:** Near roller purse (various points, along Memory Lane near the 80s section); **PC-9:** Spaceship Earth, Nautilus' (Memory Lane signs); **PC-10:** Yellow (sign along Memory Lane near the 80s section); **PC-11:** Red purse (70s buildings in the 70s section); **PC-12:** 1973 (Memory Lane sign); **PC-13:** Baloo and Mowgli from the Jungle Book (next to the check-in desk); **PC-14:** 1980 (sign along Memory Lane near 80s section); **PC-15:** CE 8055; **PC-16:** Yellow, Sky and My Little Chickadee (Behind the check-in desk); **PC-17:** 1960s (behind the check-in desk); **PC-18:** The Monorail (about halfway along the lobby opposite the check-in desk); **PC-19:** Times Computers (70s display in the lobby); **PC-20:** Andrea Gabbard (check-in desk area by characters); **PC-21:** 1954 (Memory Lane sign); **PC-22:** City of Angels soundtrack (at the very end of the check-in hall near the arcade entrance); **PC-23:** Eero Saarinen (1965 sign along Memory Lane); **PC-24:** Scott Stillinger (Next to Potato Heads on Memory Lane); **PC-25:** Corduroy Cascades (Sweet Sounds of the Seventies). (Large 8 track cassette at end of the lobby, near rooms 6101 to 6472 and Memory Lane)

Answers to Port Orleans — **PO-1:** Playground (to the west of building #2 in French Quarter); **PO-2:** Sidewinder (to the west of building #2 in French Quarter); **PO-3:** 8 spitting frogs (between buildings #6 and #7 in French Quarter); **PO-4:** Costumed revelers, presumably for Mardi Gras (French Quarter check-in area); **PO-5:** Ceiling of Sassagoula Floatworks Factory (French Quarter food court); **PO-6:** A rudder (Near lobby of Riverside); **PO-7:** Magnolia Terrace (Magnolia Bend Section of Riverside); **PO-8:** Mickey's head (Riverside Mill food court, near the bakery); **PO-9:** 'spirits and victuals' (lounge near lobby at Riverside); **PO-10:** Behind Acadian House (northeast corner of Riverside); **PO-11:** 1251 Dixie Dr., Lake Buena Vista, FL (on the arcade certificate near the Medicine Show Arcade entrance at Riverside); **PO-12:** 1875 (near lobby at Riverside); **PO-13:** 40 persons (pool rules sign near the wading pool on Ol' Man Island at Riverside); **PO-14:** 300 persons (sign outside Floatworks at French Quarter); **PO-15:** 1885 (sign on bridge at Riverside); **PO-16:** 15 minutes (spa rules sign located at the hot tub, which is hidden behind the pool bar if you're at the main pool at French Quarter); **PO-17:** A young man (the story of Ol' Man Island, near the theme park at Riverside); **PO-18:** Warranted, Full-weight, Full-strength (sign in Fulton's Market at Riverside); **PO-19:** A banjo (on building #5 at French Quarter); **PO-20:** 9:00 pm (bar in the lobby of Riverside); **PO-21:** 2251 Orleans Dr (elevator certificate at French Quarter); **PO-22:** Building #2 (on the signs for building #2)

Answers to Polynesian — **PL-1:** Two drums (resort entrance); **PL-2:** 1971; **PL-3:** Maui Mickey's; **PL-4:** #7–1294; **PL-5:** Wyland Galleries; **PL-6:** Tinkerbell; **PL-7:** Red; **PL-8:** Mikala Canoe Club; **PL-9:** 'Ohana restaurant (second floor of Great Ceremonial House); **PL-10:** Restrooms; **PL-11:** Shower before entering; **PL-12:** Roseate Spoonbill; **PL-13:** 3 feet; **PL-14:** Tonga, Fiji, Rarotonga (sign on second floor between 'Ohana and Kona Cafe); **PL-15:** 7:00 am—10:00 pm (sign outside the Hawaii building); **PL-16:** Huey, Dewey, and Louie; **PL-17:** Palau Customs; **PL-18:** Stitch (menu board located near Kona Isle Coffee); **PL-19:** The Soul (sign on directory of the monorail entrance); **PL-20:** Hand Carved Coconut (specialty drink at Barefoot Bar); **PL-21:** Merry Monarch (signs across from the 'Ohana podium); **PL-22:** February First (Kona Cafe)

Answers to Saratoga Springs — **SS-1:** Seven pictures (Carriage House); **SS-2:** It's a carousel horse (Carriage House); **SS-3:** Old Duck 'High Rocks (sign along the hallway leading to the Turf Club lounge); **SS-4:** Eight Mickeys (They have Mickey, Minnie, Goofy and related symbols on them (on the wall on left as you enter the Turf Club); **SS-5:** Lake Buena Vista (west of Carriage House); **SS-6:** High Rock Springs (signs by pool); **SS-7:** 24 hours (sign by pool); **SS-8:** Bikes and surries (on Broadway Street); **SS-9:** quiet pool (Congress Park); **SS-10:** Pool bar (sign near pool); **SS-11:** They have Mickey, Minnie, Goofy and related symbols on them (on the wall on left as you enter the Turf Club); **SS-12:** Union Avenue (signs, resort maps); **SS-13:** 89.1 FM; **SS-14:** Three fish (on Broadway Street); **SS-15:** Samson (display in The Artist's Palette store); **SS-16:** Pig (The Artist's Palette); **SS-17:** 300 (display in The Artist's Palette store); **SS-18:** Five (on left wall of vestibule as you enter the Carriage House from drop-off); **SS-19:** 133rd (guest laundry near arcade); **SS-20:** Adelphi Hotel (picture across from kid's TV area near check-in desk); **SS-21:** Four horses (picture across from kid's TV area near check-in desk)

Answers to Swan and Dolphin — **SD-1:** Blue and yellow; **SD-2:** Four swans (Swan); **SD-3:** Four swans (Swan); **SD-4:** Twelfth floor (Swan); **SD-5:** Two dolphin fish (top of Dolphin resort); **SD-6:** Two dolphins (Dolphin, Lobby Level on third floor); **SD-7:** Blue (Dolphin entrance); **SD-8:** Merchandise (Dolphin, Lobby Level on third floor); **SD-9:** Seal (playground near Grotto Pool); **SD-10:** Dolphins at the Dolphin (Main Level, first floor of Dolphin); **SD-11:** 9:00 am—3:00 pm, Monday–Friday (by the swan elevators); **SD-12:** Japan Travel Desk (Dolphin); **SD-13:** 43 persons (sign near arcade door, first floor of Dolphin); **SD-14:** No (Swan); **SD-15:** Grotto Pool (between Swan and Dolphin); **SD-16:** Swan boats (between Swan and Dolphin); **SD-17:** Enchanted Tiki Room (Swan lobby between check-in desk and gift shop); **SD-18:** Dolphin Fountain (on Tubbi's Buffeteria (Main Level, first floor of Dolphin); **SD-19:** Absolut Level, Blue (Swan); **SD-20:** Video game arcade (near Tubbi's Buffeteria at the Swan, first floor); **SD-21:** 1500 Epcot Resorts Way (sign on elevators at Dolphin); **SD-22:** Mickey Mouse (main lodge lobby)

Answers to Wilderness Lodge — **WL-1:** Bear Chief (main lodge lobby); **WL-2:** Bus stop #1 (sign at bus depot); **WL-3:** Eight bells (outside south door of main lodge building); **WL-4:** Cutter Federal (main lodge lobby); **WL-5:** Mickey Mouse (main lodge lobby — 6' main lodge lobby); **WL-6:** Lincoln Logs (off main lodge lobby); **WL-7:** A birdcage (Villas lobby); **WL-8:** Moose (Iron Spike Room, first floor of Villas); **WL-9:** Fire Rock Geyser (resort maps, signs); **WL-10:** Silver Creek Falls (signs in courtyard); **WL-11:** 19th century (on the table in the Iron Spike Room, first floor of Villas); **WL-12:** An entrance to Territory Lounge (off main lodge lobby); **WL-13:** Mickey Mouse (Iron Spike Room, first floor of Villas); **WL-14:** The Wilderness Lodge Villas (Villas lobby); **WL-15:** #704 (first floor of Villas); **WL-16:** Roger Broggie (on fourth floor overlooking the lobby); **WL-17:** Paleozoic (on fourth floor overlooking the lobby); **WL-18:** Emma Nevada (Iron Spike Room, first floor of Villas); **WL-19:** pulling to the sun, moon, and stars from a box to light the darkened world (main lobby); **WL-20:** on mat at entrance to Territory Lounge (off main lodge lobby)

Answers to Yacht & Beach Club — **YB-1:** Mickey Mouse (laundry at Yacht Club near marina); **YB-2:** 1657 (lobby of Yacht Club); **YB-3:** 20 minutes (sign in laundry, near marina); **YB-4:** Mickey Mouse (laundry at Yacht Club near marina); **YB-5:** 934-3260 (sign outside salon, between Yacht & Beach Club); **YB-6:** Ages 4—12 (sign at Sandcastle Club at Beach Club); **YB-7:** Two candles (lobby of Beach Club); **YB-8:** Beach Club Marketplace (off lobby of Beach Club); **YB-9:** Yacht (sign outside salon); **YB-10:** Lucht, Ollie, and Water (outside of the Yacht Club gallery eatery); **YB-11:** The Spanker (kiddie pool signs); **YB-12:** Four feet (between Yacht & Beach Club); **YB-13:** Shirt and shoes required (near Yachtsman Steakhouse at Yacht Club); **YB-14:** Seven boats (convention center to the north of the Yacht Club); **YB-15:** Rose (Beach Club Villas); **YB-16:** Three balloons; Two yellow and one pink/ white striped (off lobby of Beach Club); **YB-17:** Samuel Hanscomb (model ship in Yacht Club lobby); **YB-18:** Larry Carr (award plaque in the Yacht Club lobby, by the ATM); **YB-19:** 72 (flag display outside of Fittings & Fairings at Beach Club); **YB-20:** Amaretto, Kahlua, Bailey's, and Pina Colada mix (on drink menu at Hurricane Hanna's); **YB-21:** Sonoma (map in Martha's Vineyard at Beach Club)

Answers to Photos Under Treasure Chest — **RE-A:** Coronado Springs (behind registration desk); **RE-B:** Caribbean Beach Resort (above Grab N' Go at Old Port Royale food court); **RE-C:** Saratoga Springs (detail of painting behind registration desk); **RE-D:** BoardWalk (on ceiling of painting at Screen Door store); **RE-E:** Wilderness Lodge (on covered walkway between Lodge and Villas)

Under the Treasure Chest

Where in the Resorts can you find these five images?

(Answers are inside the treasure chest, of course!)

RE-A

RE-B

RE-C

RE-D

RE-E

Treasure Chest #7
Disney Cruise

Open chest (tear perforation) to view the Disney Cruise answers.

Answers to Disney Magic — **DM-1:** Two buttons; **DM-2:** The Walter E. Disney Suite (deck 8 midship, port side); **DM-3:** Rockin' Bar D, Sessions and Diversions (deck 3 forward); **DM-4:** Goofy's Galley (deck 9 aft, starboard side); **DM-5:** Crew Members Only Please (deck 6 forward, port side); **DM-6:** Castaway Cay (deck 4 forward staircase); **DM-7:** Blue (deck 4 forward, port side); **DM-8:** A Traffic Light (deck 3 forward); **DM-9:** Captain Mickey (deck 3 forward); **DM-10:** Monopoly (deck 3 forward); **DM-11:** Quartermasters (deck 9 midship, starboard side); **DM-12:** Behind Guest Services desk (deck 3 midship, deck 3 aft); **DM-13:** 1998 (deck 3 forward); **DM-14:** Yellow (deck 9 aft); **DM-15:** Disney Cruise Line logo (deck 3 forward); **DM-16:** Banana bunches (deck 3 aft); **DM-17:** Ace of Hearts (decks 3 and 4 aft staircase); **DM-18:** Pinocchio's (deck 9 midship by Goofy Pool); **DM-19:** Roses with fallen petals (deck 3 midship); **DM-20:** Row J (deck 5 aft); **DM-21:** Mickey and Minnie (Disney Magic ship bow (visible from off ship); **DM-22:** Vista Spa (sign outside spa on deck 9 forward); **DM-23:** red points aft, blue points forward (decks 1, 2, 5, 6, 7, and 8); **DM-24:** aft staircase between decks 9 and 10; **DM-25:** The Magic News and Dispatch (behind midship elevators on deck 6); **DM-26:** Christmas Coral (staircase closest to the shore excursions desk); **DM-27:** Firelocker 4 (deck 1 midship); **DM-28:** 8530 (deck 8 midship, starboard side); **DM-29:** 40 (on print in deck 8 midship elevator lobby); **DM-30:** Huey, Dewey and Louie (staircase closest to Guest Services); **DM-31:** How to Dance (forward staircase between decks 6 and 7); **DM-32:** Three tables (deck 3 forward); **DM-33:** Sun and waves (deck 9 aft); **DM-34:** Peter Pan (deck 5 midship); **DM-37:** Bridge of Harmony (left picture on aft staircase of decks 4 and 5); **DM-38:** Mickey Mouse (deck 6 midship mural in newspaper headline); **DM-39:** 1938 (decks 7 and 8 midship staircase); **DM-40:** Donald Duck's clothing (on railing in the middle left of the mural on deck 6 midship); **DM-41:** 1942 (decks 5 and 6 forward staircase); **DM-42:** March 14th, 1980 (poster in first booth to the right as you enter Rockin' Bar D from the midship entrance); **DM-43:** Tri-circle Mickey symbol in steelwork (deck 10 forward); **DM-44:** Goofy (decks 5 and 6 aft staircase); **DM-45:** deck 4 aft (starboard side, by boat launching station 3 sign)

Answers to Disney Wonder — **DW-1:** Two Dolphins (deck 9 forward elevator lobby); **DW-2:** 48 inches or 122 cm. (printed on side of pool, deck 9 midship); **DW-3:** Drink, fries, burger, and hot dog (deck 9 aft by Mickey pool); **DW-4:** Ariel The Little Mermaid (deck 3 midship); **DW-5:** Beach blanket, surfboard, and kite (deck 9 aft elevator lobby); **DW-6:** A fish (above the blue number plaques, placed on the wall beside the stateroom door); **DW-7:** Beach blankets (deck 9 aft); **DW-8:** His shoes (deck 9 aft); **DW-9:** Blue (on Pinocchio's Pizzeria sign on deck 9 midship); **DW-10:** Outlook Bar sign (deck 10 midship); **DW-11:** Playing a harp (mural on back wall of restaurant, deck 3 midship); **DW-12:** Glass (atrium on decks 3-5 midship); **DW-13:** An octopus (sign on deck 3 midship, starboard side); **DW-14:** Palm trees and pineapples (deck 3 aft); **DW-15:** A grand piano (deck 3 aft); **DW-16:** Pirate hats (high on wall in Mickey Mates, deck 4 midship); **DW-17:** deck 1 forward (ship maps, deck diagrams); **DW-18:** Steamboat Willie (Mickey) (ship's bow as seen from off-ship); **DW-19:** Mickey Mouse (deck 4 midship); **DW-20:** Entryway to Parrot Cay (deck 3 aft); **DW-21:** Red thunderbolts (deck 9 midship, starboard side); **DW-22:** Venice Marghera Yard at Fincantieri Cantieri Navali Italiani S.p.A. (plaque between Goofy Pool and Quiet Cove Pool on deck 9 midship); **DW-23:** Gas pump in Route 66 (deck 10 midship); **DW-24:** A old-fashioned movie camera or movie projector (deck 4 midship); **DW-25:** Four: three guest pools on deck 9 and a crew member pool on deck 5 forward (you can see the crew member pool by going to deck 10 forward and looking down); **DW-26:** A sailboat and six signal flags—extra points if you know that the flags spell out DISNEY (deck 4 midship); **DW-27:** Three: one aft, one midship, and one forward (deck 4 deck diagrams); **DW-28:** Deck 1 aft is only accessible by stairway or elevator); **DW-29:** °6 (deck 4 aft); **DW-30:** Mickey Mouse (deck 4 midship); **DW-31:** Passage between Oceaneer Club and Lab for the kids (deck 5 midship, starboard side of atrium); **DW-32:** Triton's (deck 3 midship); **DW-33:** In display case between Mickey's Mates and Treasure Ketch (deck 4 midship); **DW-34:** photos of Beatles and Disney characters (entrance to Aloft, deck 10); **DW-35:** Port side (It's under one of the large portholes in Route 66 on deck 3 midship); **DW-36:** Appears on the 3-D deck plans near Preludes (atrium on deck 3 midship, starboard side); **DW-37:** Inside Animator's Palate (deck 4 aft, port side); **DW-38:** On right wall after you enter Diversions (deck 3 forward); **DW-39:** Wall of Route 66 (deck 3 forward); **DW-40:** A Zephyr (!"Z"ephyr alphabet picture on deck 5, port side); **DW-41:** Golden Mickeys (shown in Walt Disney Theatre, deck 4 forward); **DW-42:** Goofy (Mickeys Mates, deck 4 midship); **DW-43:** Wall of Route 66 (deck 3 forward)

Answers to Castaway Cay — **CC-1:** Messages in a bottle (front of Post Office); **CC-2:** A hot dog (photo op on way to family beach); **CC-3:** Mickey, Pluto, Donald, and Goofy (seating area near Cookie's BBQ); **CC-4:** 6 minutes (sign posted near Scuttle Cove tram stop); **CC-5:** A band-aid (navigational signpost near Scuttle Cove); **CC-6:** Donald Duck (navigational sign near Scuttle Cove tram stop); **CC-7:** Green (sign above snorkel gear rental shop); **CC-8:** Mickey's head (snorkel trail map near Gill's Fins • Boats); **CC-9:** License plates (near family beach); **CC-10:** Capt. Tom McAlpin (sign on Conched Out Bar by family beach); **CC-11:** Mens' restrooms and womens' restrooms (painted on sign of restrooms across from Palm Central Station tram stop); **CC-12:** Castaway Jo's Games (near teen beach); **CC-13:** Lightning bolts (southeast end of air strip near Palm Central Station tram stop); **CC-14:** The skeletal remains of a giant whale, sunken treasures, and the secret of youth (sign on way to family beach); **CC-15:** 15–11 3/4" (sign near Mt. Rustmore); **CC-16:** 12 Front Street (sign on far wall of Conched Out bar); **CC-17:** Manager of "Mail by Sea" (sign on front of Post Office); **CC-18:** M. Ouimet (sign on She Sells Sea Shells shop near family beach); **CC-19:** A rare butterfly collection (painted on side of crate next to restrooms across from Palm Central Station tram stop); **CC-20:** 71 (mounted on front of Post Office near dock); **CC-21:** Discovery Tents (sign near Scuttle Cove); **CC-22:** In rafters of Pop's Props (seating area near Cookie's BBQ); **CC-23:** Free car wash (painted on north side of Pump House 1 near dock); **CC-24:** Whopper (photo op on way to family beach); **CC-25:** "Sharks, barracuda, jellyfish, sea lice, sea anemone, fire coral, etc. Danger -- Please stay off rocks!" (caution sign posted at beach); **CC-26:** A doctor (sign on the bike path near massage cabanas)

Answers to Photos Under the Treasure Chest — **DCL-A:** Hanging from chandeliers in Parrot Cay; **DCL-B:** Above entrance to gangway at Port Canaveral terminal; **DCL-C:** Hat on fish at "Big Catch" photo opportunity on Castaway Cay; **DCL-D:** QuarterMasters arcade sign on deck 9 midship; **DCL-E:** Column decoration at Parrot Cay

Under the Treasure Chest

Where onboard the Disney Cruise
can you find these five images?

(Answers are inside the treasure chest,
of course!)

DCL-A

DCL-B

DCL-C

DCL-D

DCL-E

Treasure Chest #8
Water Parks

Open chest (tear perforation) to view the Water Parks answers.

Answers to Typhoon Lagoon — **TL-1:** Miss Tilly (name is on side of boat, also mentioned in various locations throughout park and on maps); **TL-2:** Surf's Up (sign at the entrance area); **TL-3:** Leaning Palms (sign at Leaning Palms eatery); **TL-4:** Lagoona Gator (shack at the beach area of the Surf Pool); **TL-5:** Three (you can count without riding); **TL-6:** Sharkus Gigantus (sign by the Shark Reef attraction); **TL-7:** Red (Shark Reef); **TL-8:** 407-WDW-PLAY (Brochure and signs in entrance area); **TL-9:** 3 feet (painted on sides of Castaway Creek); **TL-10:** Every 30 minutes (can be seen and heard from almost everywhere in park); **TL-11:** "Your Friends From the Tropics" are now called Crush 'N' Gusher (seen on billboard at Crush 'N' Gusher—northeast of Surf Pool); **TL-12:** Certain and watery doom (on signs as you enter the park); **TL-13:** Surfin Reptile (shack at the beach area of the Surf Pool); **TL-14:** Work (Typhoon Boatworks behind the Surf Pool); **TL-15:** ME9943Y (painted on boat at shop); **TL-16:** 3 foot 6 inches (painted on side of pool); **TL-17:** Manatee Marine Supply Co. (Typhoon Boatworks behind the Surf Pool); **TL-18:** Sailors (sign at the boat wash in the children's activity area); **TL-19:** "Safen Sound, Florida" (on park map at park entrance); **TL-20:** Lagoona Gator (movie poster on the back wall of the Board Room); **TL-21:** One of the slides on Crush 'N' Gusher (northeast of Surf Pool); **TL-22:** Little Surfer Gator (back wall of the board room at the beach area of the Surf Pool); **TL-23:** Catch Basin of Humunga Cowabunga (sign near the pearl factory)

Answers to Blizzard Beach — **BB-1:** Pulling Santa's sleigh (roof of building at park entrance); **BB-2:** An inner tube, scarf, and skis boots with skis—he was also wearing a hat but it fell off (signs with logos, guidemaps, statue); **BB-3:** Button (near park entrance); **BB-4:** Summit Plummet (guidemaps, signs); **BB-5:** Three flags (top of Summit Plummet); **BB-6:** Tike's Peak (kids area); **BB-7:** Eight (visible from many points around the park); **BB-8:** Mickey Ice Cream Bar (for sale at various points around the park); **BB-9:** The Downhill Double Dipper (times are displayed at bottom of slide); **BB-10:** Mt. Gushmore (guidemaps, signs); **BB-11:** Ice Gator (guidemaps, signs, statue near park entrance); **BB-12:** One slide (the enclosed slide is limited to single riders); **BB-13:** 120 Feet (guidemaps, signs); **BB-14:** Sleigh (on sign at photo op near park entrance); **BB-15:** 90 feet (on Mt. Gushmore sign); **BB-16:** Palm trees (just under Summit Plummet); **BB-17:** Skis (chairlift to Summit Plummet); **BB-18:** In the leaky, little cabin (on Cross Country Creek behind Summit Plummet); **BB-19:** Lottawatta Lodge (three rocks above the fireplace qualify as a Hidden Mickey); **BB-20:** Joe Blow (Summit Plummet queue area); **BB-21:** In the rock ledge (above Melt Away Bay)

Answers to Photos Under Treasure Chest — **WP-A:** Top of Board House near Surf Pool (Typhoon Lagoon); **WP-B:** Let's Go Slurpin' sign (Typhoon Lagoon); **WP-C:** Snowman Daddy at entrance (Blizzard Beach); **WP-D:** Sun in letter "B" of welcome sign (Blizzard Beach); **WP-E:** Hammerhead Fred on the Shark Reef building (Typhoon Lagoon)

Use this space to write answers to your own treasure hunts, keep track of scores, or just keep notes.

ANSWERS—NO PEEKING BEFORE PLAY

Under the Treasure Chest

Where in the Disney water parks can you find these five images?

(Answers are inside the treasure chest, of course!)

WP-A

WP-B

WP-C

WP-D

WP-E